PENGUIN

ROCHESTER: SEI

JOHN WILMOT, 2ND EARL OF ROCHESTER (1647–80) has been called one of the last Metaphysical poets and one of the first of the Augustans. Lyric poet, satirist, dramatist and a leading member of the 'merry gang' surrounding Charles II, he was born at Ditchley in Oxfordshire, succeeding his father when he was eleven. He was educated at Wadham College, Oxford, and on the Grand Tour of France and Italy (1661–4). At the age of eighteen he tried to abduct the heiress Elizabeth Malet and, despite the resistance of her family and a delay of eighteen months during which Rochester fought in the naval wars against the Dutch, she married him. Subsequently his time was divided between periods of domesticity with Lady Elizabeth and his four children in Oxfordshire and fashionable life in London with, among other mistresses, the actress Elizabeth Barry, and his riotous male friends, who included the Duke of Buckingham, the Earl of Dorset and Sir Charles Sedley. The best of his poetry is satire: *Artemisa to Chloe* (a satire on love), *A Satyr against Mankind* and *An Allusion to Horace* (a satire on Dryden). He also wrote more frankly about sex than anyone in English before the twentieth century. Marvell admired him, Dryden, Swift and Pope were influenced by him, and he continues to make an impression on poets today.

FRANK H. ELLIS is Mary Augusta Jordan Professor Emeritus at Smith College in Northampton, Massachusetts. His books include *Swift's Discourse* (1967), *Twentieth Century Interpretations of Robinson Crusoe* (1969), *Poems on Affairs of State, 1697–1714* (2 vols. 1970, 1975), *Swift vs. Mainwaring* (1985) and *Sentimental Comedy: Theory and Practice* (1990).

JOHN WILMOT
EARL OF ROCHESTER
Selected Works

Edited by FRANK H. ELLIS

PENGUIN BOOKS

PENGUIN BOOKS

Published by the Penguin Group
Penguin Books Ltd, 80 Strand, London WC2R ORL, England
Penguin Group (USA) Inc., 375 Hudson Street, New York, New York 10014, USA
Penguin Books Australia Ltd, 250 Camberwell Road, Camberwell, Victoria 3124, Australia
Penguin Books Canada Ltd, 10 Alcorn Avenue, Toronto, Ontario, Canada M4V 3B2
Penguin Books India (P) Ltd, 11 Community Centre, Panchsheel Park, New Delhi – 110 017, India
Penguin Group (NZ), cnr Airborne and Rosedale Roads, Albany, Auckland 1310, New Zealand
Penguin Books (South Africa) (Pty) Ltd, 24 Sturdee Avenue, Rosebank 2196, South Africa

Penguin Books Ltd, Registered Offices: 80 Strand, London WC2R ORL, England

www.penguin.com

John Wilmot, Earl of Rochester, *The Complete Works* first published 1994
This abridged and revised selection first published 2004
1

Set in Monotype Ehrhardt
Typeset by Rowland Phototypesetting Ltd, Bury St Edmunds, Suffolk
Printed in England by Clays Ltd, St Ives plc

Contents

Introduction

The reader of Rochester today needs a lot of '*Negative Capability*', or willingness to sit down 'in uncertainties, mysteries, doubts, without any irritable reaching after fact and reason'.* Rochester is an ironist and irony makes a writer say more than he may be aware of saying. One of his contemporary readers complained that 'although [Rochester] does not say a single word of what he actually thinks, he compels you to believe every word he says' (Hamilton 1930, 235). And she may have been right, for Rochester is also an illusionist. 'He took pleasure to disguise himself . . . meerly for diversion, he would go about in odd shapes, in which he acted his part so naturally, that even those who were on the secret . . . could perceive nothing by which he might be discovered' (Burnet 1680, 27–8). So except in his letters and in his *causeries* with Burnet, 'fact and reason' may be in short supply, but Rochester's literary remains deserve to be read as free-standing works of art, not as autobiography. 'Not . . . *a single word* of what he actually thinks' is an obvious exaggeration, but Rochester's verse does not take us very far into the 'mysteries' of his psyche.

Rochester's verse also deserves to be heard. Alliteration, assonance, functional dissonance, comic rhyme, obviously delight him and the sound component of his verse will delight any reader attending to it. Rochester's verse will also reward a microscopic reading. When I finally figured out how to scan ''cause 'tis the very WORST thing they can do' (29.29),† or when I finally got the point of the stanzas' tumescence in *A Song of a Young Lady. To her Ancient Lover* (45–6), or when the full glory of Charles Stuart's foreign policy: 'Peace is his aim' (17.8) – dramatized by one of Charles's casual mistresses playing the part of Peace in a court performance of

* John Keats, *Letters*, ed. Maurice Buxton Forman (1935), 72.

†Two sets of figures, in parentheses, separated by a point, represent page and line numbers in this edition; one set represents page numbers only.

John Crowne's *Calisto* – finally burst upon me, I could almost feel Rochester's hand reaching down from heaven and patting the monkey on the head. 'There is nothing as good as Rochester, even when he is not writing lyrics, until . . .? (Let the student determine when)' (Pound 1934, 145).

Rochester himself was not a closet Puritan, as some of his biographers have made out. He was an atheist; he tried to 'fortifie his Mind . . . by dispossessing it all he could of the belief or apprehensions of Religion' (Burnet 1680, 15). And he was an equally uncompromising hedonist: ''tis still better to be pleased than not' (71.2). He celebrated pleasure, by which he meant 'the free use of Wine and Women' (Burnet 1680, 38–9). He not only practised debauchery, he advocated debauchery, 'framing Arguments for Sin, making Proselytes to it, and writing Panegyricks upon Vice' (Parsons 1680, 9). Some readers may come away with the feeling that Rochester has gone far beyond decorum, even beyond cynicism, into a frightening vision of things exactly as they are. ''Tis your choice', he warns, 'whether you'll read or no'.*

F.H.E.

An Epistolary Essay from M. G. to O. B. upon their Mutual Poems, l. 34, in John Wilmot, Earl of Rochester, *The Complete Works*, ed. Frank H. Ellis (1994), 207.

Table of Dates

10 April 1647	John Wilmot born in his mother's house at Ditchley, Oxfordshire, the second but first surviving son of Henry Wilmot, Baron Wilmot of Adderbury, near Banbury, Oxfordshire (created 1st Earl of Rochester on 13 December 1652 at St Germain-en-Laye, France) and his second wife, Ann St John, daughter of Sir John St John of Lydiard Tregoze, 1st Bart.
February 1658	Succeeds as 2nd Earl of Rochester upon his father's death in Ghent.
18 January 1660– 9 September 1661	Attends Wadham College, Oxford; by virtue of his noble birth created M.A. *filius nobilis*.
February 1661	Awarded a pension of £500 a year by Charles II.
21 November 1661– 25 December 1664	Travels on the Continent with a tutor appointed by Charles II, Dr Andrew Balfour M.D.
1 October 1664	Sighted in Venice.
26 October 1664	Signs guest-book at University of Padua.
25 December 1664	Received by Charles II at Whitehall Palace bearing a letter from Charles's sister, Henrietta Anne, Duchesse d'Orléans, sister-in-law of Louis XIV.
26 May 1665	Fails to abduct Elizabeth Malet, the 'melancholy heiress' who wrote poetry; imprisoned in the Tower for three weeks.
6 July 1665	Assigned by Charles II to sea duty in the second Dutch War; distinguishes himself at Bergen (August 1665) and Solebay (September 1665) and in St James's Fight (July 1666).

31 October 1665	Awarded a free gift from Charles II of £750.
21 March 1666	Appointed gentleman of the bedchamber to Charles II with a pension of £1,000) a year for life and lodgings in Whitehall Palace.
July 1666	Commissioned captain of horse in the British army.
29 January 1667	Marries Elizabeth Malet, said to be worth £2,500 a year, and occupies Adderbury.
29 July 1667	Summoned by royal writ to his seat in the House of Lords, although a minor.
28 February 1668	Appointed gamekeeper for Oxfordshire.
16 February 1669	Boxes Tom Killigrew's ear in the King's presence, an act of lese-majesty, but is pardoned.
12 March 1669	Travels to Paris with a letter from Charles II to Henrietta Anne; remains in Paris until July 1669.
30 April 1669	First child, Anne Wilmot, baptized.
22 November 1669	Forced by illness to decline a duel with John Sheffield, Earl of Mulgrave.
January 1671	Second child, Charles Wilmot, baptized.
27 May–13 July 1671	Meets John Dryden at Windsor, reads and amends Dryden's comedy *Marriage à la Mode*, and acceps Dryden's dedication of the published play.
Summer 1672	Living at Enmore, his wife's estate in Somerset.
30 October 1672	Appointed deputy lord lieutenant of Somerset.
22 March 1673	Ordered by House of Lords not to pursue his intended duel with Robert Constable, Viscount Dunbar.
13 July 1674	Third child, Elizabeth Wilmot, baptized.
1675–6	Trains Elizabeth Barry, the 'most important actress of her time', for the stage.
4 January 1675	Charles II approves construction of 'a small building in His Majesties Privie Garden' adjoining Charles's laboratory, as a chemistry laboratory for Rochester.

24 January 1675	Appointed master and keeper of the King's hawks.
January–February 1675	Stages at Court an amateur production of John Crowne's extravaganza, *Calisto; or, The Chaste Nimph*, with the young princesses in leading roles.
27 February 1675	Appointed ranger of Woodstock Park, Oxfordshire, and in May 1675 occupies the High Lodge.
25 June 1675	'in a frolick after a rant' smashes the King's pyramidal chronometer in the Privy Garden.
Winter 1675–6	Living at Adderbury.
January 1676	Fourth and last child, Malet Wilmot, baptized.
February 1676	Seriously ill; reported dead and buried.
11 March 1676	George Etherege's *The Man of Mode, or Sir Fopling Flutter* (in which Thomas Betterton created the role of Dorimant (Rochester) and Elizabeth Barry the role of Mrs Loveit (Dorimant's mistress)) opens at Dorset Garden Theatre.
18 June 1676	Goes into hiding after a drunken brawl in Epsom, a suburb of London, in which a man, Downs, was killed.
Late 1676	Banished from Court.
13 April 1677	Petitions Charles II for grants of estates in Ireland.
August 1677	Charles II and his favourite, George Villiers, Duke of Buckingham, 'very merry one night at Lord Rochester's lodgings' in Whitehall.
October 1677	Duke of Buckingham and his beagle pack visit Rochester at the High Lodge.
November 1677	Elected alderman of Taunton, Somerset, near Elizabeth Malet's estate at Enmore.
December 1677	Elizabeth Clerk, Rochester's daughter by Elizabeth Barry, born; in Rochester's will she is left £40 a year on good security.
April 1678	'very ill and very penitent'.
October 1679	After reading the first volume of Gilbert

	Burnet's *History of the Reformation in England* (1679–1714), summons Burnet, who had been dismissed as a royal chaplain and forbidden the Court, and who subsequently became Rochester's first biographer (1680) and Bishop of Salisbury (1689).
March 1680	Accepts a challenge from Edward Seymour, a privy councillor and late speaker of the House of Commons, who fails to appear on the appointed ground.
March 1680	Joins the King and court at the races in Newmarket.
March 1680	When Parliament is prorogued, retires to High Lodge.
April 1680	'wounded both in Body and Mind', seeks instruction from Burnet, who takes credit for Rochester's supposed reconciliation with the Church of England.
26 July 1680	Dies at High Lodge.
c. December 1682	Nathaniel Lee's *The Princess of Cleves* opens at Dorset Garden, in which Rochester is elegized as Count Rosidore: 'He was the Spirit of Wit – and had such an art in guilding his Failures, that it was hard not to love his faults.'

Further Reading

Bibliography

Johannes Prinz, *John Wilmot Earl of Rochester His Life and Writings* (Leipzig, 1927).

George Wasserman, *Samuel Butler and the Earl of Rochester. A Reference Guide* (Boston, 1986).

Biography

Robert Parsons, *A Sermon Preached at the Funeral of the Rt Honorable John Earl of Rochester* (Oxford, 1680).

Gilbert Burnet, *Some Passages of the Life and Death of the Right Honourable John Earl of Rochester* (London, 1680).

Vivian de S. Pinto, *Rochester: Portrait of a Restoration Poet* (London, 1935), rptd. as *Enthusiast in Wit. A Portrait of John Wilmot Earl of Rochester 1647–1680* (Lincoln, Nebraska, 1962). The standard biography.

Graham Greene, *Lord Rochester's Monkey* (New York, 1974). Written in 1930 and published without substantial revision.

Jeremy Lamb, *So Idle a Rogue: the Life and Death of Lord Rochester* (London, 1993).

Commentary

David M. Vieth, *Attribution in Restoration Poetry. A Study of Rochester's Poems of 1680* (New Haven and London, 1963).

Anne Righter (later Barton), 'John Wilmot, Earl of Rochester', Chatterton Lecture, *Proceedings of the British Academy* 53 (1968), 47–69.

Rochester. The Critical Heritage, ed. David Farley-Hills (New York, 1972).

Dustin H. Griffin, *Satires against Man. The Poems of Rochester* (Berkeley, Los Angeles, London, 1973).

David Farley-Hills, *Rochester's Poetry* (Totowa, New Jersey, 1978).

Spirit of Wit. Reconsiderations of Rochester, ed. Jeremy Treglown (Hamden, Connecticut, 1982).

John Wilmot, Earl of Rochester: Critical Essays, ed. David M. Vieth (New York, 1988).

Marianne Thormählen, *Rochester: The Poems in Context* (Cambridge, 1993).

Germaine Greer, *John Wilmot, Earl of Rochester* (Horndon, 2000).

Selected Works

To His Sacred Majesty

Virtue's triumphant shrine, who dost engage
At once three kingdoms in a pilgrimage,
Which in ecstatic duty strive to come
Out of themselves as well as from their home,
5   Whilst England grows one camp and London is
Itself the nation, not metropolis,
And loyal Kent renews her arts again,
Fencing her ways with moving groves of men,
Forgive this distant homage, which doth meet
10   Your blest approach on sedentary feet.
And though my youth, not patient yet to bear
The weight of arms, denies me to appear
In steel before you, yet, Great Sir, approve
My manly wishes and more vigourous love
15   In whom a cold respect were treason to
A father's ashes, greater than to you;
Whose one ambition 'tis for to be known
By daring loyalty your Wilmot's son.

To his Mistress

I

Why dost thou shade thy lovely face? Oh, why
Does that eclipsing hand of thine deny
The sunshine of the sun's enlivening eye?

II

Without thy light, what light remains in me?
5   Thou art my life, my way; my light's in thee;
I live, I move, and by thy beams I see.

III

Thou art my life; if thou but turn away,
My life's a thousand deaths; thou art my way;
Without thee, love, I travel not but stray.

IV

10   My light thou art; without thy glorious sight
My eyes are darkened with eternal night.
My love, thou art my way, my life, my sight.

V

Thou art my way; I wander if thou fly;
Thou art my light; if hid, how blind am I.
15   Thou art my Life; if thou withdraw'st, I die.

VI

My eyes are dark and blind, I cannot see;
To whom or whither should my darkness flee
But to that light? And who's that light but thee?

VII

If that be all, shine forth and draw thee nigher;
20   Let me be bold and die for my desire:
A phoenix likes to perish in the fire.

VIII

If my puffed light be out, give leave to tine
My flameless snuff at the bright lamp of thine;
Ah! What's thy light the less for lighting mine?

IX

25   If I have lost my path, dear lover, say,
Shall I still wander in a doubtful way?
Love, shall a lamb of Israel's sheepfold stray?

X

My path is lost; my wandering step does stray;
I cannot go nor safely stay;
30   Whom should I seek but thee, my path, my way?

XI

And yet thou turn'st thy face away and fliest me,
And yet I sue for grace, and thou deniest me;
Speak, art thou angry, love, or triest me?

XII

Display those heavenly lamps or tell me why
35   Thou shad'st thy face; perhaps no eye
Can view their flames and not drop down and die.

XIII

Thou art the pilgrim's path and blind man's eye,
The dead man's life; on thee my hopes rely;
If I but them remove, I err, I die.

XIV

40 Dissolve thy sunbeams; close thy wings and stay;
See, see how I am blind and dead and stray;
Oh, thou that art my life, my light, my way.

XV

Then work thy will; if passion bid me flee,
My reason shall obey; my wings shall be
45 Stretched out no further than from me to thee.

Verses put into a Lady's Prayer-book

Fling this useless book away
And presume no more to pray;
Heaven is just and can bestow
Mercy on none but those that mercy show.
5 With a proud heart maliciously inclined
Not to increase, but to subdue mankind,
In vain you vex the gods with your petition;
Without repentance and sincere contrition
You're in a reprobate condition.
10 Phillis, to calm the angry powers
And save my soul as well as yours,
Relieve poor mortals from despair
And justify the gods that made you fair;
And in those bright and charming eyes
15 Let pity first appear, then love,
That we by easy steps may rise
Through all the joys on earth to those above.

Rhyme to Lisbon

Here's a health to Kate, our sovereign's mate,   (14)
   Of the royal house of Lisbon,
But the Devil take Hyde and the bishop beside,
   That made her bone of his bone.

Song

Give me leave to rail at you,
I ask nothing but my due,
To call you false and then to say
You shall not keep my heart a day.
5   But alas, against my will
I must be your captive still.
Ah! be kinder then, for I
Cannot change and would not die.
Kindness has resistless charms,
10 All things else but weakly move,
Fiercest anger it disarms
And clips the wings of flying Love.
Beauty does the heart invade,
Kindness only can persuade;
15 It gilds the lover's servile chain
And makes the slave grow pleased again.

From Mistress Price, Maid of Honour to Her Majesty, who sent [Lord Chesterfield] a Pair of Italian Gloves

My Lord,
   These are the gloves that I did mention
   Last night, and 'twas with the intention
   That you should give me thanks and wear them,
   For I most willingly can spare them.

5   When you this packet first do see,
       'Damn me,' cry you, 'she has writ to me;
       I had better be at Bretby still
       Than troubled with love against my will;
       Besides, this is not all my sorrow:
10   She writ today, she'll come tomorrow.'
       Then you consider the adventure
       And think you never shall content her.
           But when you do the inside see,
       You'll find things are but as they should be,
15   And that 'tis neither love nor passion,
       But only for your recreation.

Under King Charles II's Picture

I, John Roberts, writ this same,
I pasted it and plastered it and put it in a frame
In honour of my master's master, King Charles the Second by
    name.

To his more than Meritorious Wife

I am by fate slave to your will
And shall be most obedient still;
To show my love I will compose ye
For your fair finger's ring a posy,
5   In which shall be expressed my duty,
And how I'll be forever true t'ye;
With low-made legs and sugared speeches,
Yielding to your fair bum the breeches,
I'll show myself, in all I can,
Your faithful, humble servant,

10   Jan.

Rochester Extempore

And after singing Psalm the 12th
He laid his book upon the shelf.
And looked much simply like himself;
With eyes turned up, as white as ghost,
5   He cried, 'Ah Lard, ah Lard of Hosts!
I am a rascal, that thou know'st.'

Spoken Extempore to a Country Clerk after having heard him Sing Psalms

Sternhold and Hopkins had great qualms
When they translated David's psalms,
    To make the heart full glad,
But had it been poor David's fate
5   To hear thee sing, and them translate,
    By God! 'twould have made him mad.

The Platonic Lady

I could love thee till I die,
Wouldst thou love me modestly
And ne'er press, whilst I live,
For more than willingly I'd give,
5   Which should sufficient be to prove
I'd understand the art of love.
I hate the thing is called enjoyment.
Besides, it is a dull employment,
It cuts off all that's life and fire
10   From that which may be termed desire,
Just like the bee whose sting is gone
Converts the owner to a drone.
I love a youth should give me leave
His body in my arms to wreathe,

15 To press him gently and to kiss,
    To sigh and look with eyes that wish
    For what, if I could once obtain,
    I would neglect with flat disdain.
    I'd give him liberty to toy
20 And play with me and count it joy.
    Our freedom should be full complete,
    And nothing wanting but the feat.
    Let's practise then and we shall prove
    These are the only sweets of love.

Song

    As Cloris full of harmless thought
        Beneath the willows lay,
    Kind Love a comely shepherd brought
        To pass the time away.
5   She blushed to be encountered so
        And chid the amorous swain,
    But as she strove to rise and go,
        He pulled her down again.

    A sudden passion seized her heart
10   In spite of her disdain,
    She found a pulse in every part
        And love in every vein.
    'Ah, youth,' quoth she, 'what charms are these
        That conquer and surprise?
15 Ah, let me, for unless you please,
        I have no power to rise.'

    She faintly spoke and trembling lay
        For fear he should comply,
    But virgins' eyes their hearts betray
20   And give their tongues the lie.
    Thus she, who princes had denied
        With all their pompous train,
    Was in the lucky minute tried
        And yielded to a swain.

Song to Cloris

Fair Cloris in a pigsty lay,
    Her tender herd lay by her.
She slept; in murmuring gruntlings they,
Complaining of the scorching day,
5   Her slumbers thus inspire.

She dreamt, while she with careful pains
    Her snowy arms employed
In ivory pails to fill out grains,
One of her love-convicted swains
10   Thus hasting to her cried:

'Fly, nymph! Oh fly! ere 'tis too late
    A dear loved life to save,
Rescue your bosom pig from fate,
Who now expires, hung in the gate
15   That leads to Flora's cave.

'Myself had tried to set him free
    Rather than brought the news,
But I am so abhorred by thee
That ev'n thy darling's life from me
20   I know thou wouldst refuse.'

Struck with the news, as quick she flies
    As blushes to her face;
Not the bright lightning from the skies
Nor love, shot from her brighter eyes,
25   Move half so swift a pace.

This plot, it seems, the lustful slave
    Had laid against her honour,
Which not one god took care to save,
For he pursues her to the cave
30   And throws himself upon her.

Now piercèd is her virgin zone,
    She feels the foe within it;
She hears a broken, amorous groan,
The panting lover's fainting moan,
35   Just in the happy minute.

Frighted she wakes and waking frigs.
    Nature thus kindly eased
In dreams raised by her murmuring pigs
And her own thumb between her legs,
40   She's innocent and pleased.

To Corinna

What cruel pains Corinna takes
    To force that harmless frown:
When not one charm her face forsakes,
    Love cannot lose his own.

5 So sweet a face, so soft a heart,
    Such eyes so very kind,
Betray, alas, the silly art
    Virtue had ill designed.

Poor feeble tyrant, who in vain
10   Would proudly take upon her,
Against kind Nature to maintain
    Affected rules of honour.

The scorn she bears, so helpless proves
    When I plead passion to her,
15 That much she fears, but more she loves,
    Her vassal should undo her.

Song

Phillis, be gentler, I advise,
    Make up for time misspent.
When beauty on its deathbed lies,
    'Tis high time to repent.

5 Such is the malice of your fate,
    That makes you old so soon,
Your pleasure ever comes too late,
    How early e'er begun.

Think what a wretched thing is she
10   Whose stars contrive in spite,
The morning of her love should be
    Her fading beauty's night.

Then if to make your ruin more,
    You'll peevishly be coy,
15 Die with the scandal of a whore,
    And never know the joy.

May transports that can give new fire
    To stay the flying soul,
Ne'er answer you in your desire,
20   But make you yet more dull.

May raptures that can move each part
    To taste the joys above,
In all their height improved by art,
    Still fly you when you love.

[*Could I but make my wishes insolent*]

Could I but make my wishes insolent
And force some image of a false content!
But they, like me, bashful and humble grown,
Hover at distance about beauty's throne,
5 There worship and admire, and then they die,
Daring no more lay hold of her than I.
Reason to worth bears a submissive spirit,
But fools can be familiar with merit.
Who but that blundering blockhead Phaëton
10 Could e'er have thought to drive about the sun?
Just such another durst make love to you
Whom not ambition led, but dullness drew.
No amorous thought could his dull heart incline
But he would have a passion, for 'twas fine!
15 That, a new suit, and what he next must say
Runs in his idle head the livelong day.

Hard-hearted saint, since 'tis your will to be
So unrelenting pitiless to me
Regardless of a love so many years
20 Preserved 'twixt lingering hopes and awful fears
(Such fears in lovers' breasts high value claims
And such expiring martyrs feel in flames.
My hopes yourself contrived with cruel care
Through gentle smiles to lead me to despair),
25 'Tis some relief in my extreme distress
My rival is below your power to bless.

[*The gods by right of nature must possess*]

The gods by right of nature must possess
An everlasting age of perfect peace:
Far off removed from us and our affairs,
Neither approached by dangers or by cares,
5 Rich in themselves, to whom we cannot add,
Not pleased by good deeds nor provoked by bad.

To Love

O! numquam pro me satis indignate Cupido

O Love! how cold and slow to take my part,
Thou idle wanderer about my heart.
Why thy old faithful soldier wilt thou see
Oppressed in my own tents? They murder me;
5 Thy flames consume, thy arrows pierce thy friends.
Rather on foes pursue more noble ends.
Achilles' sword would generously bestow
A cure as certain, as it gave the blow.
Hunters who follow flying game give o'er
10 When the prey's caught; hope still leads on before.
We thine own slaves feel thy tyrannic blows,
Whilst thy tame hand's unmoved against thy foes.

On men disarmed how can you gallant prove,
And I was long ago disarmed by Love.
15   Millions of dull men live, and scornful maids:
We'll own Love valiant when he these invades.
Rome from each corner of the wide world snatched
A laurel, or't had been to this day thatched.
But the old soldier has his resting place,
20   And the good battered horse is turned to grass.
The harassed whore, who lived a wretch to please,
Has leave to be a bawd and take her ease.
For me then, who have freely spent my blood,
Love, in thy service and so boldly stood
25   In Celia's trenches, were't not wisely done
Ev'n to retire and live at peace at home?
No! Might I gain a godhead to disclaim
My glorious title to my endless flame,
Divinity with scorn I would forswear,
30   Such sweet, dear, tempting devils women are.
Whene'er those flames grow faint, I quickly find
A fierce, black storm pour down upon my mind.
Headlong I'm hurled like horsemen who in vain
Their fury-foaming coursers would restrain,
35   As ships, just when the harbour they attain,
Are snatched by sudden blasts to sea again,
So Love's fantastic storms reduce my heart,
Half-rescued, and the god resumes his dart.
Strike here, this undefended bosom wound,
40   And for so brave a conquest be renowned.
Shafts fly so fast to me from every part,
You'll scarce discern your quiver from my heart.
What wretch can bear a livelong night's dull rest
Or think himself in lazy slumbers blest?
45   Fool! Is not sleep the image of pale death?
There's time for rest when fate has stopped your breath.
Me may my soft-deluding dear deceive;
I'm happy in my hopes whilst I believe.
Now let her flatter, then as fondly chide.
50   Often may I enjoy, oft be denied.

With doubtful steps the god of war does move
By thy example led, ambiguous Love.
Blown to and fro like down from thy own wing,
Who knows when joy or anguish thou wilt bring?
55 Yet at thy mother's and thy slave's request,
Fix an eternal empire in my breast,
    And let th'inconstant charming sex,
    Whose wilful scorn does lovers vex,
    Submit their hearts before thy throne,
60   The vassal world is then thy own.

The Imperfect Enjoyment

Naked she lay, clasped in my longing arms,
I filled with love, and she all over charms,
Both equally inspired with eager fire,
Melting through kindness, flaming in desire;
5 With arms, legs, lips, close clinging to embrace,
She clips me to her breast and sucks me to her face.
Her nimble tongue (Love's lesser lightning) played
Within my mouth and to my thoughts conveyed
Swift orders that I should prepare to throw
10 The all–dissolving thunderbolt below.
My fluttering soul, sprung with a pointed kiss,
Hangs hovering o'er her balmy brinks of bliss,
But whilst her busy hand would guide that part
Which should convey my soul up to her heart,
15 In liquid raptures I dissolve all o'er,
Melt into sperm and spend at every pore.
A touch from any part of her had done't,
Her hand, her foot, her very look's a cunt.
Smiling, she chides in a kind, murmuring noise,
20 And from her body wipes the clammy joys,
When with a thousand kisses wandering o'er
My panting bosom, 'Is there then no more?'
She cries, 'All this to love and rapture's due,
Must we not pay a debt to pleasure too?'

25 But I, the most forlorn, lost man alive,
To show my wished obedience vainly strive,
I sigh, alas, and kiss, but cannot swive.
Eager desires confound my first intent,
Succeeding shame does more success prevent,
30 And rage at last confirms me impotent.
Ev'n her fair hand, which might bid heat return
To frozen age and make cold hermits burn,
Applied to my dead cinder warms no more
Than fire to ashes could past flames restore.
35 Trembling, confused, despairing, limber, dry,
A wishing, weak, unmoving lump I lie.
This dart of Love, whose piercing point oft tried,
With virgin blood ten thousand maids has dyed,
Which nature still directed with such art
40 That it through every cunt reached every heart;
Stiffly resolved, 'twould carelessly invade
Woman or boy, nor ought its fury stayed;
Where'er it pierced, a cunt it found or made,
Now languid lies in this unhappy hour,
45 Shrunk up and sapless like a withered flower.
Thou treacherous, base deserter of my flame,
False to my passion, fatal to my fame,
By what mistaken magic dost thou prove
So true to lewdness, so untrue to Love?
50 What oyster, cinder, beggar, common whore
Didst thou e'er fail in all thy life before?
When vice, disease, and scandal lead the way,
With what officious haste dost thou obey?
Like a rude, roaring hector in the streets
55 That scuffles, cuffs, and justles all he meets,
But if his king or country claim his aid,
The rakehell villain shrinks and hides his head;
Ev'n so thy brutal valor is displayed,
Breaks every stew, does each small whore invade,
60 But if great Love the onset does command,
Base recreant to thy prince, thou dar'st not stand.
Worst part of me and henceforth hated most,
Through all the town the common fucking post

On whom each whore relieves her tingling cunt,
65 As hogs on gates do rub themselves and grunt,
May'st thou to ravenous chancres be a prey,
Or in consuming weepings waste away.
May strangury and stone thy days attend;
May'st thou ne'er piss who didst refuse to spend
70 When all my joys did on false thee depend.
And may ten thousand abler pricks agree
To do the wronged Corinna right for thee.

On King Charles

In the isle of Great Britain long since famous grown
For breeding the best cunts in Christendom,
There reigns, and oh, long may he reign and thrive,
The easiest prince and best-bred man alive.
5 Him no ambition moves to seek renown
Like the French fool, to wander up and down
Starving his subjects, hazarding his crown.
Peace is his aim, his gentleness is such,
And love he loves, for he loves fucking much.
10 Nor are his high desires above his strength,
His sceptre and his prick are of a length;
And she that plays with one may sway the other
And make him little wiser than his brother.
I hate all monarchs and the thrones they sit on,
15 From the hector of France to the cully of Britain.
    Poor prince, thy prick, like thy buffoons at court,
It governs thee, because it makes thee sport.
'Tis sure the sauciest prick that e'er did swive,
The proudest, peremptoriest prick alive.
20 Though safety, law, religion, life lay on't,
'Twould break through all to make its way to cunt.
Restless he rolls about from whore to whore,
A merry monarch, scandalous and poor.
To Carwell, the most dear of all his dears,
25 The sure relief of his declining years,

Oft he bewails his fortune and her fate:
To love so well, and to be loved so late.
For when in her he settles well his tarse,
Yet his dull, graceless ballocks hang an arse.
30   This you'd believe, had I but time to tell y'
The pain it costs to poor, laborious Nelly,
While she employs hands, fingers, lips, and thighs,
Ere she can raise the member she enjoys.

A Ramble in St James's Park

Much wine had passed with grave discourse
Of who fucks who and who does worse,
Such as you usually do hear
From them that diet at the Bear,
5   When I, who still take care to see
Drunkenness relieved by lechery,
Went out into St James's Park
To cool my head and fire my heart.
But though St James has the honour on't,
10   'Tis consecrate to prick and cunt.
There by a most incestuous birth
Strange woods spring from the teeming earth,
For they relate how heretofore,
When ancient Pict began to whore,
15   Deluded of his assignation
(Jilting it seems was then in fashion),
Poor pensive lover in this place
Would frig upon his mother's face,
Whence rows of mandrakes tall did rise
20   Whose lewd tops fucked the very skies.
Each imitative branch does twine
In some loved fold of Aretine.
And nightly now beneath their shade
Are buggeries, rapes, and incests made.
25   Unto this all-sin-sheltering grove
Whores of the bulk and the alcove,

Great ladies, chambermaids, and drudges,
The rag-picker and heiress trudges.
Carmen, divines, great lords, and tailors,
'Prentices, pimps, poets, and jailers,
Footmen, fine fops do here arrive,
And here promiscuously they swive.
 Along these hallowed walks it was
That I beheld Corinna pass.
Whoever had been by to see
The proud disdain she cast on me
Through charming eyes, he would have swore
She dropped from heav'n that very hour,
Forsaking the divine abode
In scorn of some despairing god.
But mark what creatures women are,
So infinitely vile, when fair.
 Three knights of th'elbow and the slur
With wriggling tails made up to her.
 The first was of your Whitehall blades,
Near kin to th'Mother of the Maids,
Graced by whose favour he was able
To bring a friend to th'waiters' table,
Where he had heard Sir Edward Sutton
Say how the King loved Banstead mutton;
Since when he'd ne'er be brought to eat
By's good will any other meat.
In this, as well as all the rest,
He ventures to do like the best,
But wanting common sense, th'ingredient
In choosing well not least expedient,
Converts abortive imitation
To universal affectation.
So he not only eats and talks,
But feels and smells, sits down and walks,
Nay, looks and lives and loves by rote
In an old tawdry birthday coat.
 The second was a Gray's Inn wit,
A great inhabiter of the pit,

65   Where critic-like he sits and squints,
      Steals pocket handkerchiefs and hints
      From's neighbour and the comedy,
      To court and pay his landlady.
          The third, a lady's eldest son
70   Within few years of twenty-one,
      Who hopes from his propitious fate
      Against he comes to his estate,
      By these two worthies to be made
      A most accomplished, tearing blade.
75   One in a strain 'twixt tune and nonsense
      Cries, 'Madam, I have loved you long since,
      Permit me your fair hand to kiss';
      When at her mouth her cunt says, 'Yes'.
          In short, without much more ado,
80   Joyful and pleased away she flew
      And with these three confounded asses
      From park to hackney coach she passes;
      So a proud bitch does lead about
      Of humble curs the amorous rout,
85   Who most obsequiously do hunt
      The savory scent of salt-swol'n cunt.
      Some power more patient now relate
      The sense of this surprising fate,
      Gads! that a thing admired by me
90   Should fall to so much infamy.
      Had she picked out to rub her arse on
      Some stiff-pricked clown or well-hung parson,
      Each job of whose spermatic sluice
      Had filled her cunt with wholesome juice,
95   I the proceeding should have praised
      In hope she'd quenched a fire I raised.
      Such natural freedoms are but just:
      There's something generous in mere lust.
      But to turn damned abandoned jade
100   When neither head nor tail persuade,
      To be a whore in understanding,
      A passive pot for fools to spend in –

The devil played booty, sure, with thee
To bring a blot on infamy.
105 But why am I of all mankind
To so severe a fate designed?
Ungrateful! why this treachery
To humble, fond, believing me,
Who gave you privileges above
110 The nice allowances of love?
Did ever I refuse to bear
The meanest part your lust could spare?
When your lewd cunt came spewing home
Drenched with the seed of half the town,
115 My dram of sperm was supped up after
For the digestive surfeit water.
Full gorgèd at another time
With a vast meal of nasty slime
Which your devouring cunt had drawn
120 From porters' backs and footmen's brawn,
I was content to serve you up
My ballock-full for your grace cup;
Nor ever thought it an abuse,
While you had pleasure for excuse.
125 You that could make my heart away
For noise and colour and betray
The secrets of my tender hours
To such knight-errant paramours,
When leaning on your faithless breast,
130 Wrapped in security and rest,
Soft kindness all my powers did move,
And reason lay dissolved in love.
May stinking vapours choke your womb,
Such as the men you dote upon.
135 May your depravèd appetite,
That could in whiffling fools delight,
Beget such frenzies in your mind
You may go mad for the north wind
And fixing all your hopes upon't
140 To have him bluster in your cunt

Turn up your longing arse to th'air
And perish in a wild despair.
But cowards shall forget to rant,
Schoolboys to frig, old whores to paint;
145 The Jesuits' fraternity
Shall leave the use of buggery;
Crab-louse, inspired with grace divine,
From earthly cod to heaven shall climb;
Physicians shall believe in Jesus,
150 And disobedience cease to please us,
Ere I desist with all my power
To plague this woman and undo her.
But my revenge will best be timed
When she is married that is limed.
155 In that most lamentable state
I'll make her feel my scorn and hate,
Pelt her with scandals, truth, or lies,
And her poor cur with jealousies,
Till I have torn him from her breech,
160 While she whines like a dog-drawn bitch,
Loathed and despised, kicked out of town
Into some dirty hole alone,
To chew the cud of misery
And know she owes it all to me.
165 And may no woman better thrive
Who dares profane the cunt I swive.

Song

Love a woman? You're an ass.
'Tis a most insipid passion
To choose out for your happiness
The idlest part of God's creation.

5 Let the porter and the groom,
Things designed for dirty slaves,
Drudge in fair Aurelia's womb
To get supplies for age and graves.

Farewell, woman! I intend
10 Henceforth every night to sit
With my lewd, well-natured friend,
Drinking to engender wit.

Then give me health, wealth, mirth, and wine,
And if busy Love intrenches,
15 There's a sweet, soft page of mine
Does the trick worth forty wenches.

Seneca's Troas, *Act 2. Chorus*

After death nothing is, and nothing, death,
The utmost limit of a gasp of breath.
Let the ambitious zealot lay aside
His hopes of heaven, whose faith is but his pride;
5   Let slavish souls lay by their fear
   Nor be concerned which way nor where
   After this life they shall be hurled.
Dead, we become the lumber of the world,
And to that mass of matter shall be swept
10 Where things destroyed with things unborn are kept.
   Devouring time swallows us whole.
Impartial death confounds body and soul.
   For Hell and the foul fiend that rules
   God's everlasting fiery jails
15   (Devised by rogues, dreaded by fools),
With his grim, grisly dog that keeps the door,
   Are senseless stories, idle tales,
     Dreams, whimseys, and no more.

Tunbridge Wells

At five this morn when Phoebus raised his head
From Thetis' lap, I raised myself from bed
And mounting steed, I trotted to the waters,
The rendezvous of feigned or sickly praters,
5   Cuckolds, whores, citizens, their wives and daughters.
My squeamish stomach I with wine had bribed
To undertake the dose it was prescribed,
But turning head, a sudden noisome view
That innocent provision overthrew
10 And without drinking made me purge and spew.
Looking on t'other side, a thing I saw
Who some men said could handle sword and law.
It stalked, it stared, and up and down did strut,
And seemed as furious as a stag at rut.
15 As wise as calf it looked, as big as bully,
But handled, proved a mere Sir Nicholas Cully,
A bawling fop, a natural Nokes, and yet
He dared to censure as if he had wit.
To make him more ridiculous, in spite
20 Nature contrived the fool should be a knight.
Grant ye lucky stars this o'ergrown boy
To purchase some inspiring pretty toy
That may his want of sense and wit supply,
As buxom crab-fish do his lechery.
25 Though he alone were dismal sight enough,
His train contributed to set him off,
All of his shape, all of the self-same stuff.
In short, no malice need on him be thrown,
Nature has done the business of lampoon,
30 And in his looks his character hath shown.
Endeavouring this irksome sight to balk,
And a more irksome noise, his silly talk,
I silently slunk down to th' Lower Walk.
But often when one would Charybdis shun,
35 Down upon Scylla 'tis one's fate to run;

So here it was my cursèd fate to find
As great a fop, though of another kind,
A tall, stiff fool who walked in Spanish guise;
The buckram puppet never stirred its eyes,
40 But grave as owl it looked, as woodcock wise.
He scorned the empty talking of this mad age
And spoke all proverbs, sentences, and adage,
Can with as much solemnity buy eggs
As a cabal can talk of their intrigues,
45 A man of parts, and yet he can dispense
With the formaljty of speaking sense.
    From hence into the upper end I ran,
Where a new scene of foppery began
Among the serious and fanatic elves,
50 Fit company for none besides themselves.
Assembled thus, each his distemper told:
Scurvy, stone, strangury. Some were so bold
To charge the spleen to be their misery,
And on the wise disease bring infamy.
55 But none were half so modest to complain
Their want of learning, honesty, and brain,
The general diseases of that train.
These call themselves ambassadors of Heaven
And saucily pretend commissions given,
60 But should an Indian king, whose small command
Seldom extends above ten miles of land,
Send forth such wretched fools in an embassage,
He'd find but small effects of such a message.
Listening, I found the cob of all this rabble,
65 Pert Bayes, with his importance comfortable.
He, being raised to an archdeaconry
By trampling on religious liberty,
Was grown too great and looked too fat and jolly
To be disturbed with care or melancholy,
70 Though Marvell has enough exposed his folly.
He drank to carry off some old remains
His lazy dull distemper left in's veins.
Let him drink on, but 'tis not a whole flood
Can give sufficient sweetness to his blood

75   To make his nature or his manners good.
Importance drank too, though she'd been no sinner,
To wash away some dregs he had spewed in her.
   Next after these a foolish whining crew
Of sisters frail were offered to my view.
80   The things did talk, but th' hearing what they said
I did myself the kindness to evade.
Looking about, I saw some gypsies too
(Faith, brethren, they can cant as well as you).
Nature hath placed these wretches beneath scorn;
85   They can't be called so vile as they are born.
   Amidst the crowd next I myself conveyed,
For now were come, whitewash and paint being laid,
Mother and daughters, mistress and the maid,
And squire with wig and pantaloons displayed.
90   But ne'er could conventicle, play, or fair
For a true medley with this herd compare.
Here squires, ladies, and some say countesses,
Chandlers, egg-wives, bacon-women, seamstresses
Were mixed together, nor did they agree
95   More in their humours than their quality.
Here waiting for gallant, young damsel stood,
Leaning on cane and muffled up in hood.
The would-be wit, whose business was to woo,
With hat removed and solemn scrape of shoe
100   Advanceth bowing, then genteelly shrugs
And ruffled foretop into order tugs,
And thus accosts her, 'Madam, methinks the weather
Is grown much more serene since you came hither.
You influence the heavens; and should the sun
105   Withdraw himself to see his rays outdone,
Your brighter eyes could then supply the morn
And make a day before a day be born.'
   With mouth screwed up, conceited winking eyes,
And breasts thrust forwards, 'Lord, sir,' she replies,
110   'It is your goodness, and not my deserts,
Which makes you show this learning, wit, and parts.'
He, puzzled, bites his nail, both to display
The sparkling ring and think what next to say,

And thus breaks forth afresh, 'Madam, egad,
115 Your luck at cards last night was very bad.
At cribbage fifty-nine, and the next show
To make the game, and yet to want those two.
God damn me, madam, I'm the son of a whore
If in my life I saw the like before.'
120 To pedlar's stall he drags her, and her breast
With hearts and such-like foolish toys he dressed;
And then more smartly to expound the riddle
Of all his prattle, gives her a Scotch fiddle.
　　Tired with this dismal stuff, away I ran
125 Where were two wives with girl just fit for man,
Short-breathed, with pallid lips, and visage wan.
Some curtsies passed, and the old compliment
Of being glad to see each other, spent,
With hand in hand they lovingly did walk,
130 And one began thus to renew the talk.
'I pray, good madam, if it may be thought
No rudeness, what cause was it hither brought
Your ladyship?' She soon replying, smiled,
'We have a good estate, but have no child,
135 And I'm informed these wells will make a barren
Woman as fruitful as a cony warren.'
The first returned, 'For this cause I am come,
For I can have no quietness at home.
My husband grumbles, though we have got one,
140 This poor girl, and mutters for a son.
And this is grieved with headache pangs and throes,
Is full sixteen and never yet had those.'
She soon replied, 'Get her a husband, madam.
I married at that age and ne'er had had 'em,
145 Was just like her. Steel waters let alone,
A back of steel will bring 'em better down.'
And ten to one but they themselves will try
The same means to increase their family.
Poor foolish fribbles, who by subtlety
150 Of midwife, truest friend to lechery,
Persuaded are to be at pains and charge
To give their wives occasion to enlarge

Their silly heads. For here walk Cuff and Kick
With brawny back and legs and potent prick,
155 Who more substantially will cure thy wife,
And on her half-dead womb bestow new life.
From these the waters got the reputation
Of good assistants unto generation.
    Now warlike men were got into the throng,
160 With hair tied back, singing a bawdy song.
Not much afraid, I got a nearer view,
And 'twas my chance to know the dreadful crew.
They were cadets, that seldom can appear,
Damned to the stint of thirty pound a year.
165 With hawk on fist or greyhound led in hand,
The dogs and footboys sometimes they command.
And having trimmed a cast-off spavined horse,
With three hard-pinched-for guineas in the purse,
Two rusty pistols, scarf about the arse,
170 Coat lined with red, they here presume to swell;
This goes for captain, that for colonel.
So the Bear Garden ape on his steed mounted,
No longer is a jackanapes accounted,
But is by virtue of his trumpery then
175 Called by the name of the young gentleman.
    Bless me, thought I, what thing is man, that thus
In all his shapes he is ridiculous?
Ourselves with noise of reason we do please
In vain: humanity's our worst disease.
180 Thrice happy beasts are, who, because they be
Of reason void, are so of foppery.
Troth, I was so ashamed that with remorse
I used the insolence to mount my horse;
For he, doing only things fit for his nature,
185 Did seem to me (by much) the wiser creature.

Artemisa to Chloe.
A Letter from a Lady in the Town to a Lady in the
Country concerning the Loves of the Town

Chloe,
    In verse by your command I write,
Shortly you'll bid me ride astride and fight;
Such talents better with our sex agree
Than lofty flights of dangerous poetry.
5 Amongst the men, I mean the men of wit
(At least they passed for such before they writ),
How many bold adventurers for the bays,
Proudly designing large returns of praise,
Who durst that stormy, pathless world explore,
10 Were soon dashed back and wrecked on the dull shore,
Broke of that little stock they had before?
How would a woman's tottering bark be tossed
Where stoutest ships, the men of wit, are lost.
When I reflect on this, I straight grow wise,
15 And my own self thus gravely I advise:
Dear Artemisa, poetry's a snare;
Bedlam has many mansions, have a care:
Your muse diverts you, makes your reader sad;
You fancy you're inspired, he thinks you mad.
20 Consider too 'twill be discreetly done
To make yourself the fiddle of the town,
To find th'ill-humoured pleasure at their need,
Scorned if you fail and cursed if you succeed.
Yet like an arrant woman as I am,
25 No sooner well convinced writing's a shame,
That whore is scarce a more reproachful name
Than poetess –
As men that marry or as maids that woo
'Cause 'tis the very worst thing they can do,
30 Pleased with the contradiction and the sin,
Methinks I stand on thorns till I begin.
    You expect to hear at least what loves have passed
In this lewd town since you and I met last,

What change hath happened of intrigues, and whether
35   The old ones last, and who and who's together.
But how, my dearest Chloe, shall I set
My pen to write what I would fain forget
Or name that lost thing, love, without a tear,
Since so debauched by ill-bred customs here?
40   Love, the most generous passion of the mind,
The softest refuge innocence can find,
The safe director of unguided youth,
Fraught with kind wishes and secured by truth,
That cordial drop heaven in our cup has thrown
45   To make the nauseous draught of life go down;
On which one only blessing God might raise
In lands of atheists subsidies of praise,
For none did e'er so dull and stupid prove
But felt a god and blest his power in love.
50   This only joy for which poor we were made
Is grown, like play, to be an arrant trade:
The rooks creep in, and it has got of late
As many little cheats and tricks as that.
But what yet more a woman's heart would vex,
55   'Tis chiefly carried on by our own sex,
Our silly sex, who born like monarchs, free,
Turn gypsies for a meaner liberty
And hate restraint, though but from infamy.
They call whatever is not common, nice,
60   And deaf to nature's rules and love's advice,
Forsake the pleasures to pursue the vice.
To an exact perfection they have wrought
The action, love; the passion is forgot.
'Tis below wit, they'll tell you, to admire,
65   And ev'n without approving, they desire.
Their private wish obeys the public voice;
'Twixt good and bad, whimsey decides, not choice.
Fashions grow up for taste, at forms they strike,
They know what they would have, not what they like.
70   Bovey is a beauty, if some few agree
To call him so; the rest to that degree
Affected are, that with their ears they see.

Where I was visiting the other night
Comes a fine lady with her humble knight,
75 Who had prevailed on her by her own skill
At his request though much against his will
To come to London.
As the coach stopped, we heard her voice, more loud
Than a great-bellied woman's in a crowd,
80 Telling her knight that her affairs require
He for some hours obsequiously retire.
I think she was ashamed to have him seen
(Hard fate of husbands): the gallant had been,
Though a diseased, hard-favoured fool, brought in.
85 'Dispatch,' says she, 'that business you pretend,
That beastly visit to your drunken friend.
A bottle ever makes you look so fine,
Methinks I long to smell you stink of wine.
Your country drinking breath's enough to kill,
90 Sour ale corrected with a lemon peel.
Prithee, farewell, we'll meet again anon.'
The necessary thing bows and is gone.
She flies upstairs, and all the haste does show
That fifty antic postures will allow,
95 And then bursts out, 'Dear madam, am not I
The altered'st creature breathing, let me die;
I find myself ridiculously grown
Embarrassée with being out of town,
Rude and untaught like any Indian queen,
100 My country nakedness is strangely seen.
How is love governed, love that rules the state,
And pray, who are the men most worn of late?
When I was married, fools were *à la mode*,
The men of wit were then held *incommode*,
105 Slow of belief and fickle in desire,
Who, ere they'll be persuaded, must inquire
As if they came to spy, not to admire.
With searching wisdom, fatal to their ease,
They'll still find out why what may, should not please,
110 Nay, take themselves for injured if we dare
Make them think better of us than we are,

And if we hide our frailties from their sights,
Call us deceitful jilts and hypocrites.
They little guess, who at our arts are grieved,
115 The perfect joy of being well deceived,
Inquisitive as jealous cuckolds grow;
Rather than not be knowing, they will know
What being known creates their certain woe.
Women should these of all mankind avoid,
120 For wonder by clear knowledge is destroyed.
Woman, who is an arrant bird of night,
Bold in the dusk before a fool's dull sight,
Should fly when reason brings the glaring light.
But the kind, easy fool, apt to admire
125 Himself, trusts us; his follies all conspire
To flatter his and favour our desire.
Vain of his proper merit, he with ease
Believes we love him best who best can please.
On him our common, gross, dull flatteries pass,
130 Ever most joyful when most made an ass:
Heavy to apprehend, though all mankind
Perceive us false, the fop concerned is blind,
Who doting on himself,
Thinks everyone that sees him of his mind.
135 These are true women's men.' Here forced to cease
For want of breath, not will to hold her peace,
She to the window runs, where she had spied
Her much esteemed dear friend, the monkey, tied.
With forty smiles, as many antic bows
140 As if 't had been the lady of the house,
The dirty, chattering monster she embraced,
And made it this fine tender speech at last:
'Kiss me, thou curious miniature of man,
How odd thou art, how pretty, how japan!
145 Oh, I could live and die with thee.' Then on
For half an hour in compliment she run.
    I took this time to think what nature meant
When this mixed thing into the world she sent,
So very wise, yet so impertinent:

150 One who knew everything, who 'twas thought fit
    Should be a fool through choice, not want of wit,
    Whose foppery without the help of sense
    Could ne'er have rose to such an excellence.
    Nature's as lame in making a true fop
155 As a philosopher; the very top
    And dignity of folly we attain
    By curious search and labour of the brain,
    By observation, counsel, and deep thought:
    God never made a coxcomb worth a groat;
160 We owe that name to industry and arts,
    An eminent fool must be a fool of parts.
    And such a one was she, who had turned o'er
    As many books as men, loved much, read more,
    Had a discerning wit; to her was known
165 Everyone's fault and merit but her own.
    All the good qualities that ever blest
    A woman so distinguished from the rest,
    Except discretion only, she possessed.
        And now, 'Monsieur dear Pug,' she cries, 'adieu',
170 And the discourse broke off, does thus renew:
    'You smile to see me, whom the world perchance
    Mistakes to have some wit, so far advance
    The interest of fools that I approve
    Their merit more than men's of wit, in love.
175 But in our sex too many proofs there are
    Of such whom wits undo and fools repair.
    This in my time was so received a rule
    Hardly a wench in town but had her fool;
    The meanest common slut, who long was grown
180 The jest and scorn of every pit buffoon,
    Had yet left charms enough to have subdued
    Some fop or other fond to be thought lewd.
    Foster could make an Irish lord a Nokes,
    And Betty Morris had her City cokes.
185 A woman's ne'er so ruined but she can
    Be still revenged on her undoer, man:
    How lost soe'er, she'll find some lover more
    A lewd, abandoned fool than she's a whore.

'That wretched thing, Corinna, who had run
190 Through all the several ways of being undone,
Cozened at first by love, and living then
By turning the too dear-bought trick on men:
Gay were the hours and winged with joy they flew,
When first the town her early beauty knew;
195 Courted, admired, and loved, with presents fed
Youth in her looks and pleasure in her bed,
Till fate or her ill angel thought it fit
To make her dote upon a man of wit,
Who found 'twas dull to love above a day,
200 Made his ill-natured jest, and went away.
Now scorned by all, forsaken, and oppressed,
She's a *memento mori* to the rest,
Diseased, decayed, to take up half a crown
Must mortgage her long scarf and manteau gown.
205 Poor creature, who unheard of as a fly
In some dark hole must all the winter lie,
And want and dirt endure a whole half year
That for one month she tawdry may appear.
In Easter term she gets her a new gown,
210 When my young master's worship comes to town,
From pedagogue and mother just set free,
The heir and hopes of a great family,
Who with strong ale and beef the country rules,
And ever since the Conquest have been fools.
215 And now with careful prospect to maintain
This character, lest crossing of the strain
Should mend the booby breed, his friends provide
A cousin of his own for his fair bride.
And thus set out
220 With an estate, no wit, and a young wife,
The solid comforts of a coxcomb's life,
Dunghill and pease forsook, he comes to town,
Turns spark, learns to be lewd, and is undone.
Nothing suits worse with vice than want of sense:
225 Fools are still wicked at their own expense.
This o'ergrown schoolboy lost Corinna wins
And at first dash to make an ass begins,

Pretends to like a man who has not known
The vanities nor vices of the town.
230 Fresh in his youth and faithful in his love,
Eager of joys which he does seldom prove;
Healthful and strong, he does no pains endure
But what the fair one he adores can cure;
Grateful for favours, does the sex esteem,
235 And libels none for being kind to him;
Then of the lewdness of the town complains,
Rails at the wits and atheists, and maintains
'Tis better than good sense, than power, than wealth
To have a love untainted, youth, and health.
240 The unbred puppy, who had never seen
A creature look so gay or talk so fine,
Believes, then falls in love, and then in debt,
Mortgages all, ev'n to the ancient seat,
To buy his mistress a new house for life,
245 To give her plate and jewels, robs his wife;
And when to th' height of fondness he is grown,
'Tis time to poison him, and all's her own.
Thus meeting in her common arms his fate,
He leaves her bastard heir to his estate,
250 And, as the race of such an owl deserves,
His own dull lawful progeny he starves.
Nature who never made a thing in vain,
But does each insect to some end ordain,
Wisely contrived kind keeping fools, no doubt,
255 To patch up vices men of wit wear out.'
Thus she ran on two hours, some grains of sense
Mixed with whole volleys of impertinence.
      But now 'tis time I should some pity show
To Chloe, since I cannot choose but know
260 Readers must reap the dullness writers sow.
By the next post such stories I will tell
As joined with these, shall to a volume swell,
As true as heaven, more infamous than hell;
But now you're tired, and so am I.
                                        Farewell.

Timon. A Satyr

A. What, Timon, does old age begin t'approach
That thus thou droop'st under a night's debauch?
Hast thou lost deep to needy rogues on tick
Who ne'er could pay, and must be paid next week?

5 TIMON Neither, alas, but a dull dining sot
Seized me i'th' Mall, who just my name had got;
He runs upon me, cries, 'Dear rogue, I'm thine,
With me some wits of thy acquaintance dine.'
I tell him I'm engaged, but as a whore

10 With modesty enslaves her spark the more,
The longer I denied, the more he pressed.
At last I ev'n consent to be his guest.

He takes me in his coach and, as we go,
Pulls out a libel of a sheet or two,

15 Insipid as the praise of pious queens
Or Shadwell's unassisted former scenes,
Which he admired and praised at every line.
At last it was so sharp it must be mine.
I vowed I was no more a wit than he,

20 Unpractised and unblessed in poetry.
A song to Phillis I perhaps might make,
But never rhymed but for my pintle's sake.
I envied no man's fortune nor his fame,
Nor ever thought of a revenge so tame.

25 He knew my style, he swore, and 'twas in vain
Thus to deny the issue of my brain.
Choked with his flattery, I no answer make,
But silent, leave him to his dear mistake,
Which he by this had spread o'er the whole town

30 And me with an officious lie undone.
Of a well-meaning fool I'm most afraid,
Who sillily repeats what was well said.
But this was not the worst. When he came home,
He asked, 'Are Sedley, Buckhurst, Savile come?'

35 No, but there were above Halfwit and Huff,
Kickum and Dingboy. 'Oh, 'tis well enough.

They're all brave fellows,' cries mine host, 'Let's dine,
I long to have my belly full of wine.
They wil! both write and fight, I dare assure you,
40   They're men *tam Marte quam Mercurio.*'
I saw my error, but 'twas now too late:
No means nor hopes appear of a retreat.
Well, we salute, and each man takes his seat.
'Boy,' says my sot, 'is my wife ready yet?'
45   A wife, good gods! a fop and bullies too!
For one poor meal what must I undergo?
    In comes my lady straight; she had been fair,
Fit to give love and to prevent despair,
But age, beauty's incurable disease,
50   Had left her more desire than power to please.
As cocks will strike although their spurs be gone,
She with her old blear eyes to smite begun.
Though nothing else, she (in despite of time)
Preserved the affectation of her prime:
55   However you begun, she brought in love
And hardly from that subject would remove.
We chanced to speak of the French king's success;
My lady wondered much how heaven could bless
A man that loved two women at one time,
60   But more how he to them excused his crime.
She asked Huff if love's flame he never felt.
He answered bluntly, 'Do you think I'm gelt?'
She at his plainness smiled, then turned to me,
'Love in young minds precedes ev'n poetry.
65   You to that passion can no stranger be,
But wits are given to inconstancy.'
She had run on, I think, till now, but meat
Came up, and suddenly she took her seat.
I thought the dinner would make some amends,
70   When my good host cries out, 'You're all my friends,
Our own plain fare and the best tierce the Bull
Affords I'll give you and your bellies full.
As for French kickshaws, sillery, and champagne,
Ragouts and fricassees, in troth, we've none.'

75   'Here's a good dinner towards,' thought I, when straight
      Up comes a piece of beef, full horseman's weight,
      Hard as the arse of Moseley, under which
      The coachman sweats as ridden by a witch,
      A dish of carrots, each of them as long
80   As tool that to fair countess did belong,
      Which her small pillow could not so well hide
      But visitors his flaming head espied.
      Pig, goose, and capon followed in the rear,
      With all that country bumpkins call good cheer,
85   Served up with sauces, all of 'eighty-eight,
      When our tough youth wrestled and threw the weight.
      And now the bottle briskly flies about,
      Instead of ice, wrapped up in a wet clout.
      A brimmer follows the third bit we eat,
90   Small beer becomes our drink and wine our meat.
      The table was so large that in less space
      A man might, safe, six old Italians place:
      Each man had as much room as Porter, Blunt,
      Or Harris had in Cullen's bushel cunt.
95   And now the wine began to work. Mine host
      Had been a colonel; we must hear him boast,
      Not of towns won, but an estate he lost
      For the King's service, which indeed he spent
      Whoring and drinking, but with good intent.
100   He talked much of a plot, and money lent
      The King in Cromwell's time. My lady, she
      Complained our love was coarse, our poetry
      Unfit for modest ears; small whores and players
      Were of our hare-brained youth the only cares,
105   Who were too wild for any virtuous league,
      Too rotten to consummate the intrigue.
      Falkland she praised, and Suckling's easy pen,
      And seemed to taste their former parts again.
      Mine host drinks to the best in Christendom,
110   And decently my lady quits the room.
          Left to ourselves, of several things we prate,
      Some regulate the stage and some the state.

Halfwit cries up my lord of Orrery,
'Ah, how well Mustapha and Zanger die!
115   His sense so little forced that by one line
You may the other easily divine:
> *And which is worse, if any worse can be,*
> *He never said one word of it to me.*
There's fine poetry! You'd swear 'twere prose,
120   So little on the sense the rhymes impose.'
'Damn me!' says Dingboy, 'In my mind, God's wounds,
Etherege writes airy songs and soft lampoons
The best of any man; as for your nouns,
Grammar, and rules of art, he knows 'em not,
125   Yet writ two talking plays without one plot.'
Huff was for Settle, and *Morocco* praised,
Said rumbling words, like drums, his courage raised:
> *Whose broad-built bulks the boist'rous billows bear,*
> *Safi and Salé, Mogador, Oran,*
130   > *The famed Arzile, Alcazar, Tetuan.*
'Was ever braver language writ by man?'
Kickum for Crowne declared, said in romance
He had outdone the very wits of France:
'Witness *Pandion* and his *Charles the Eight*,
135   Where a young monarch, careless of his fate,
Though foreign troops and rebels shock his state,
Complains another sight afflicts him more,
Viz.
> *The queen's galleys rowing from the shore,*
> *Fitting their oars and tackling to be gone,*
140   > *Whilst sporting waves smiled on the rising sun.*
"Waves smiling on the sun!" I'm sure that's new,
And 'twas well thought on, give the Devil his due.'
Mine host, who had said nothing in an hour,
Rose up and praised *The Indian Emperour*:
145   > *As if our old world modestly withdrew,*
> *And here in private had brought forth a new.*
'There are two *lines*! Who but he durst presume
To make th' old world a new withdrawing room,
Where of another world she's brought to bed!
150   What a brave midwife is a laureate's head!

But pox of all these scribblers. What d'you think,
Will Souches this year any champagne drink?
Will Turenne fight him?' 'Without doubt,' says Huff,
'When they two meet, their meeting will be rough.'
155 'Damn me!' says Dingboy, 'The French cowards are;
They pay, but th' English, Scots, and Swiss make war.
In gaudy troops at a review they shine,
But dare not with the Germans battle join.
What now appears like courage, is not so;
160 'Tis a short pride which from success does grow.
On their first blow they'll shrink into those fears
They showed at Crécy, Agincourt, Poitiers.
Their loss was infamous; honour so stained
Is by a nation not to be regained.'
165 'What they were then, I know not, now they're brave.
He that denies it lies and is a slave,'
Says Huff and frowned. Says Dingboy, 'That do I!'
And at that word at t'other's head let fly
A greasy plate, when suddenly they all
170 Together by the ears in parties fall.
Halfwit with Dingboy joins, Kickum with Huff.
Their swords were safe, and so we let them cuff
Till they, mine host, and I had all enough.
Their rage once over, they begin to treat,
175 And six fresh bottles must the peace complete.
I ran downstairs with a vow nevermore
To drink beer-glass and hear the hectors roar.

A Dialogue between Strephon and Daphne

STREPHON Prithee now, fond fool, give o'er;
             Since my heart is gone before,
             To what purpose should I stay?
             Love commands another way.

5 DAPHNE Perjured swain, I knew the time
             When dissembling was your crime.

In pity now employ that art
Which first betrayed, to ease my heart.

STREPHON Women can with pleasure feign;
10   Men dissemble still with pain.
        What advantage will it prove
        If I lie, who cannot love?

DAPHNE Tell me then the reason why
        Love from hearts in love does fly;
15   Why the bird will build a nest
        Where he ne'er intends to rest?

STREPHON Love, like other little boys,
        Cries for hearts, as they for toys,
        Which, when gained, in childish play
20   Wantonly are thrown away.

DAPHNE Still on wing, or on his knees,
        Love does nothing by degrees:
        Basely flying when most prized,
        Meanly fawning when despised,

25   Flattering or insulting ever,
        Generous and grateful never:
        All his joys are fleeting dreams,
        All his woes severe extremes.

STREPHON Nymph, unjustly you inveigh;
30   Love, like us, must fate obey.
        Since 'tis Nature's law to change,
        Constancy alone is strange.

        See the heavens in lightnings break,
        Next in storms of thunder speak,
35   Till a kind rain from above
        Makes a calm – so 'tis in love.

        Flames begin our first address,
        Like meeting thunder we embrace;
        Then you know the showers that fall
40   Quench the fire, and quiet all.

DAPHNE   How should I these showers forget,
         'Twas so pleasant to be wet;
         They killed love, I knew it well,
         I died all the while they fell.

45   Say at least what nymph it is
         Robs my breast of so much bliss?
         If she's fair, I shall be eased;
         Through my ruin you'll be pleased.

STREPHON Daphne never was so fair,
50   Strephon scarcely so sincere.
         Gentle, innocent, and free,
         Ever pleased with only me.

         Many charms my heart enthrall,
         But there's one above them all:
55   With aversion she does fly
         Tedious, trading, constancy.

DAPHNE   Cruel shepherd! I submit;
         Do what Love and you think fit.
         Change is fate, and not design;
60   Say you would have still been mine.

STREPHON Nymph, I cannot; 'tis too true,
         Change has greater charms than you.
         Be, by my example, wise;
         Faith to pleasure sacrifice.

65 DAPHNE Silly swain, I'll have you know,
         'Twas my practice long ago:
         Whilst you vainly thought me true,
         I was false in scorn of you.

         By my tears, my heart's disguise,
70   I thy love and thee despise.
         Womankind more joy discovers
         Making fools than keeping lovers.

The Fall

How blest was the created state
Of man and woman ere they fell,
Compared to our unhappy fate;
We need not fear another hell.

5   Naked beneath cool shades they lay;
Enjoyment waited on desire.
Each member did their wills obey,
Nor could a wish set pleasure higher.

But we poor slaves to hope and fear
10 Are never of our joys secure;
They lessen still as they draw near,
And none but dull delights endure.

Then, Cloris, while I duty pay
The nobler tribute of a heart,
15 Be not you so severe to say
You love me for a frailer part.

The Mistress

An age in her embraces passed
    Would seem a winter's day
Where life and light with envious haste
    Are torn and snatched away.

5 But oh, how slowly minutes roll
    When absent from her eyes
That feed my love, which is my soul,
    It languishes and dies.

For then no more a soul but shade,
10   It mournfully does move
And haunts my breast, by absence made
    The living tomb of love.

You wiser men, despise me not,
   Whose lovesick fancy raves
15 On shades of souls and heaven knows what:
   Short ages live in graves.

Whene'er those wounding eyes so full
   Of sweetness you did see,
Had you not been profoundly dull,
20   You had gone mad like me.

Nor censure us, you who perceive
   My best beloved and me
Sigh and lament, complain and grieve,
   You think we disagree.

25 Alas! 'tis sacred jealousy,
   Love raised to an extreme,
The only proof 'twixt her and me
   We love and do not dream.

Fantastic fancies fondly move
30   And in frail joys believe,
Taking false pleasure for true love,
   But pain can ne'er deceive.

Kind jealous doubts, tormenting fears,
   And anxious cares, when past,
35 Prove our hearts' treasure fixed and dear,
   And make us blest at last.

A Song

Absent from thee I languish still;
Then ask me not when I return.
The straying fool 'twill plainly kill
To wish all day, all night to mourn.

5 Dear, from thine arms then let me fly,
That my fantastic mind may prove
The torments it deserves to try
That tears my fixed heart from my love.

When wearied with a world of woe
10 To thy safe bosom I retire
Where love and peace and truth does flow,
May I contented there expire,

Lest, once more wandering from that heaven,
I fall on some base heart unblest,
15 Faithless to thee, false, unforgiven,
And lose my everlasting rest.

A Song of a Young Lady. To her Ancient Lover

Ancient person, for whom I
All the flattering youth defy,
Long be it ere thou grow old,
Aching, shaking, crazy, cold.
5 But still continue as thou art,
Ancient person of my heart.

On thy withered lips and dry,
Which like barren furrows lie,
Brooding kisses I will pour
10 Shall thy youthful heat restore,
Such kind showers in autumn fall
And a second spring recall,
Nor from thee will ever part,
Ancient person of my heart.

15 Thy nobler part, which but to name
In our sex would be counted shame,
By Age's frozen grasp possessed,
From his ice shall be released,
And, soothed by my reviving hand,
20 In former warmth and vigour stand.
All a lover's wish can reach,
For thy joy my love shall teach.

And for thy pleasure shall improve
All that art can add to love.
25　Yet still I love thee without art,
Ancient person of my heart.

A Satyr against Mankind

Were I (who to my cost already am)
One of those strange, prodigious creatures, man
A spirit free to choose for my own share
What case of flesh and blood I pleased to wear,
5　I'd be a dog, a monkey, or a bear,
Or anything but that vain animal
Who is so proud of being rational.
The senses are too gross, and he'll contrive
A sixth to contradict the other five,
10　And before certain instinct, will prefer
Reason, which fifty times for one does err;
Reason, an *ignis fatuus* in the mind,
Which leaves the light of nature, sense, behind,
Pathless and dangerous wandering ways it takes
15　Through error's fenny bogs and thorny brakes,
Whilst the misguided follower climbs with pain
Mountains of whimseys heaped in his own brain;
Tumbling from thought to thought, falls headlong down
Into doubt's boundless sea, where, like to drown,
20　Books bear him up awhile and make him try
To swim with bladders of philosophy.
In hope still to o'ertake th'escaping light,
The vapour dances in his dazzled sight
Till spent, it leaves him to eternal night.
25　Then Old Age and Experience, hand in hand,
Lead him to death and make him understand,
After a search so painful and so long,
That all his life he has been in the wrong.
Huddled in dirt, the reasoning engine lies,
30　Who was so proud, so witty, and so wise.

Pride drew him in, as cheats their bubbles catch,
And made him venture to be made a wretch.
His wisdom did his happiness destroy,
Aiming to know that world he should enjoy.
35 And wit was his vain, frivolous pretense
Of pleasing others at his own expense.
For wits are treated just like common whores;
First they're enjoyed and then kicked out of doors.
The pleasure past, a threatening doubt remains
40 That frights th'enjoyer with succeeding pains.
Women and men of wit are dangerous tools
And ever fatal to admiring fools.
Pleasure allures, and when the fops escape,
'Tis not that they're belov'd but fortunate,
45 And therefore what they fear, at heart they hate.
But now methinks some formal band and beard
Takes me to task. Come on, sir, I'm prepared.
    'Then, by your favour, anything that's writ
Against this gibing, jingling knack called wit
50 Likes me abundantly, but you'll take care
Upon this point, not to be too severe.
Perhaps my muse were fitter for this part,
For I profess I can be very smart
On wit, which I abhor with all my heart.
55 I long to lash it in some sharp essay,
But your grand indiscretion bids me stay
And turns my tide of ink another way.
What rage ferments in your degenerate mind
To make you rail at reason and mankind?
60 Blest, glorious man, to whom alone kind heaven
An everlasting soul hath freely given,
Whom his great maker took such care to make
That from himself he did the image take
And this fair frame in shining reason dressed
65 To dignify his nature above beast;
Reason, by whose aspiring influence
We take a flight beyond material sense,
Dive into mysteries, then soaring pierce
The flaming limits of the universe,

70 Search heaven and hell, find out what's acted there,
And give the world true grounds of hope and fear!'
      'Hold, mighty man,' I cry, 'all this we know
From the pathetic pen of Ingelo,
From Patrick's *Pilgrim*, Stillingfleet's replies,
75 And 'tis this very reason I despise
This supernatural gift that makes a mite
Think he's the image of the infinite,
Comparing his short life, void of all rest,
To the eternal and the ever blest,
80 This busy, puzzling stirrer up of doubt
That frames deep myst'ries and then finds them out,
Filling with frantic crowds of thinking fools
Those reverend bedlams, colleges and schools,
Borne on whose wings, each heavy sot can pierce
85 The limits of the boundless universe;
So charming ointments make an old witch fly
And bear a crippled carcass through the sky.
'Tis this exalted power, whose business lies
In nonsense and impossibilities,
90 This made a whimsical philosopher
Before the spacious world his tub prefer,
And we have modern, cloistered coxcombs who
Retire to think, 'cause they have nought to do.
But thoughts were given for action's government;
95 Where action ceases, thought's impertinent.
Our sphere of action is life's happiness,
And he who thinks beyond thinks like an ass.
Thus, whilst against false reasoning I inveigh,
I own right reason, which I would obey,
100 That reason which distinguishes by sense
And gives us rules of good and ill from thence,
That bounds desires with a reforming will
To keep them more in vigour, not to kill.
Your reason hinders, mine helps to enjoy,
105 Renewing appetites yours would destroy.
My reason is my friend, yours is a cheat:
Hunger calls out, my reason bids me eat,
Perversely, yours your appetite does mock;

This asks for food, that answers, "What's o'clock?"
110 This plain distinction, sir, your doubt secures:
'Tis not true reason I despise, but yours.'
    Thus I think reason righted, but for man
I'll ne'er recant; defend him if you can.
For all his pride and his philosophy,
115 'Tis evident beasts are in their degree
As wise at least and better far than he.
Those creatures are the wisest who attain
By surest means the ends at which they aim.
If therefore Jowler finds and kills his hares
120 Better than Meres supplies committee chairs,
Though one's a statesman, t'other but a hound,
Jowler in justice would be wiser found.
    You see how far man's wisdom here extends,
Look next if human nature makes amends.
125 Whose principles most gen'rous are and just,
And to whose morals you would sooner trust,
Be judge yourself, I'll bring it to the test
Which is the basest creature, man or beast?
Birds feed on birds, beasts on each other prey,
130 But savage man alone does man betray.
Pressed by necessity, they kill for food;
Man undoes man to do himself no good.
With teeth and claws by nature armed, they hunt
Nature's allowance to supply their want,
135 But man with smiles, embraces, friendship, praise,
Most humanly his fellow's life betrays,
With voluntary pains works his distress,
Not through necessity but wantonness.
For hunger or for love they bite and tear,
140 Whilst wretched man is still in arms for fear.
For fear he arms and is of arms afraid,
From fear to fear successively betrayed,
Base fear, the source whence his best actions came,
His boasted honour and his dear-bought fame,
145 The lust of power to which he's such a slave
And for the which alone he dares be brave,
To which his various projects are designed,

Which makes him generous, affable, and kind,
For which he takes such pains to be thought wise,
150 And screws his actions in a forced disguise,
Leads a most tedious life in misery
Under laborious, mean hypocrisy.
Look to the bottom of this vast design,
Wherein man's wisdom, power, and glory join:
155 The good he acts, the ill he does endure,
'Tis all from fear, to make himself secure.
Merely for safety, after fame they thirst,
For all men would be cowards if they durst,
And honesty's against all common sense:
160 Men must be knaves, 'tis in their own defence.
Mankind's dishonest; if you think it fair
Amongst known cheats to play upon the square,
You'll be undone.
Nor can weak truth your reputation save:
165 The knaves will all agree to call you knave.
Wronged shall he live, insulted o'er, oppressed,
Who dares be less a villain than the rest.
Thus here you see what human nature craves:
Most men are cowards, all men should be knaves.
170 The difference lies, as far as I can see,
Not in the thing itself, but the degree,
And all the subject matter of debate
Is only, Who's a knave of the first rate?
     All this with indignation have I hurled
175 At the pretending part of the proud world,
Who, swollen with selfish vanity, devise
False freedoms, holy cheats, and formal lies
Over their fellow slaves to tyrannize.
     But if in court so just a man there be
180 (In court, a just man, yet unknown to me)
Who does his needful flattery direct,
Not to oppress and ruin, but protect;
Since flattery, which way soever laid,
Is still a tax on that unhappy trade,
185 If so upright a statesman you can find,
Whose passions bend to his unbiased mind,

Who does his arts and policies apply
To raise his country, not his family,
Nor while his pride owned avarice withstands,
190   Receives close bribes from friends' corrupted hands;
Is there a churchman who on God relies,
Whose life, his faith and doctrine justifies;
Not one blown up with vain, prelatic pride,
Who for reproof of sins does man deride;
195   Whose envious heart makes preaching a pretense,
With his obstreperous, saucy eloquence,
Dares chide at kings and rail at men of sense;
Who from his pulpit vents more peevish lies,
More bitter railings, scandals, calumnies,
200   Than at a gossiping are thrown about
When the good wives get drunk and then fall out;
None of that sensual tribe whose talents lie
In avarice, pride, sloth, and gluttony,
Who hunt good livings but abhor good lives,
205   Whose lust exalted to that height arrives
They act adultery with their own wives,
And ere a score of years completed be,
Can from the lofty pulpit proudly see
Half a large parish their own progeny;
210   Nor doting bishop who would be adored
For domineering at the council board,
A greater fop in business at fourscore,
Fonder of serious toys, affected more
Than the gay, glittering fool at twenty proves
215   With all his noise, his tawdry clothes, and loves;
But a meek, humble man of modest sense,
Who, preaching peace, does practise continence,
Whose pious life's a proof he does believe
Mysterious truths which no man can conceive;
220   If upon earth there dwell such God-like men,
I'll here recant my paradox to them,
Adore those shrines of virtue, homage pay,
And with the rabble world their laws obey.
     If such there are, yet grant me this at least,
225   Man differs more from man than man from beast.

Plain Dealing's Downfall

Long time Plain Dealing in the haughty town,
Wand'ring about, though in a threadbare gown,
At last unanimously was cried down.

When almost starved, she to the country fled
5 In hopes though meanly she should there be fed
And tumble nightly on a pea-straw bed.

But Knavery, knowing her intent, took post
And rumoured her approach through every coast,
Vowing his ruin that should be her host.

10 Frighted at this, each rustic shut his door,
Bid her be gone and trouble him no more,
For he that entertained her must be poor.

At this, grief seized her, grief too great to tell,
When weeping, sighing, fainting, down she fell,
15 Whilst Knavery, laughing, rung her passing bell.

[*What vain, unnecessary things are men!*]

What vain, unnecessary things are men!
How well we do without 'em! Tell me then
Whence comes that mean submissiveness we find
This ill-bred age has wrought on womankind?
5 Fall'n from the rights their sex and beauties gave
To make men wish, despair, and humbly crave,
Now 'twill suffice if they vouchsafe to have.
To the Pall Mall, playhouse, and the drawing room,
Their women fairs, these women coursers come
10 To chaffer, choose, and ride their bargains home.
At the appearance of an unknown face
Up steps the arrogant, pretending ass,
Pulling by th'elbow his companion, Huff,
Cries, 'Look, by God that wench is well enough,

15 Fair and well-shaped, good lips and teeth, 'twill do;
   She shall be tawdry for a month or two
   At my expense, be rude and take upon her,
   Show her contempt of quality and honour,
   And with the general fate of errant woman
20 Be very proud awhile, then very common.'
   Ere bear this scorn, I'd be shut up at home,
   Content with humouring myself alone,
   Force back the humble love of former days
   In pensive madrigals and ends of plays,
25 When, if my lady frowned, th'unhappy knight
   Was fain to fast and lie alone that night.
   But whilst th'insulting wife the breeches wore,
   The husband took her clothes to give his whore,
   Who now maintains it with a gentler art;
30 Thus tyrannies to commonwealths convert.
   Then after all, you find, whate'er we say,
   Things must go on in their lewd, natural way.
   Besides, the beastly men we daily see
   Can please themselves alone as well as we.
35 Therefore, kind ladies of the town, to you
   For our stol'n, ravished men we hereby sue.
   By this time you have found out, we suppose,
   That they're as arrant tinsel as their clothes,
   Poor broken properties that cannot serve
40 To treat such persons so as they deserve.
   Mistake us not, we do not here pretend
   That like young sparks you can condescend
   To love a beastly playhouse creature. Foh!
   We dare not think so meanly of you. No,
45 'Tis not the player pleases but the part;
   She may like Rollo who despises Hart.
   To theatres, as temples, you are brought
   Where Love is worshipped and his precepts taught.
   You must go home and practise, for 'tis here,
50 Just as in other preaching places, where
   Great eloquence is shown 'gainst sin and papists
   By men who live idolators and atheists.

These two were dainty trades indeed, could each
Live up to half the miracles they teach;
55 Both are a

Consideratus, Considerandus

What pleasures can the gaudy world afford?
What true delights does teeming nature hoard
In her great store-house where she lays her treasure?
Alas, 'tis all the shadow of a pleasure;
5 No true content in all her works are found,
No solid joys in all earth's spacious round
For labouring man, who toils himself in vain,
Eagerly grasping what creates his pain.
How false and feeble, nay scarce worth a name
10 Are riches, honour, power, and babbling fame.
Yet 'tis, for these men wade through seas of blood,
And bold in mischief, storm to be withstood,
Which when obtained breed but stupendous fear,
Strife, jealousies, and sleep-disturbing care.
15 No beam of comfort, not a ray of light
Shines thence, to guide us through fate's gloomy night,
But lost in devious darkness, there we stay,
Bereft of reason in an endless way.
Virtue's the solid good, if any be;
20 'Tis that creates our true felicity,
Though we despise, contemn, and cast it by
As worthless or our fatal'st enemy
Because our darling lusts it dare control
And bound the rovings of the madding soul.
25 Therefore in garments poor, it still appears
And sometimes naked, it no garments wears,
Shunned by the great and worthless thought by most,
Urged to be gone or wished for ever lost.
Yet it is loath to leave our wretched coast,
30 But in disguise does here and there intrude,
Striving to conquer base ingratitude,

And boldly ventures now and then to shine,
So to make known it is of birth divine,
But clouded oft, it like the lightning plays,
35 Loosing as soon as seen its pointed rays.
Which scarceness makes those that are weak in wit
For virtue's self admire its counterfeit,
With which damned hypocrites the world delude
As we on Indians glass for gems intrude.

Scene i. Mr Dainty's Chamber

Enter Dainty in his nightgown, singing.

DAINTY *J'ai l'amour dans le cœur et la rage dans les os.* I am
confident I shall never sleep again. And t'were no great
matter, if it did not make me look thin. For naturally I hate
to be so long absent from myself, as one is in a manner
5 those seven dull hours he snores away. And yet methinks
not to sleep till the sun rise is an odd effect of my disease
and makes the night tedious without a woman. Reading
would relieve me, but books treat of other men's affairs,
10 and to me that's tiresome. Besides, I seldom have candle.
But I am resolved to write some love passages of my own
life. They will make a pretty novel. And when my boy buys
a link, it shall burn by me when I go to bed, while I divert
myself with reading my own story, which will be pleasant
15 enough. Boy!
Enter Boy.
BOY Sir?
DAINTY Who knocked at door just now? Was it some woman?
BOY Mistress Manners's maid, sir, with a posset for you.
DAINTY And you never brought her up, you rascal? How can
20 you be so ill-bred and belong to me? See who knocks there.
Some other woman?   *Exit Boy*
Mistress Manners's fondness for me is very useful, for besides
the good things she always sends me, and money I borrow
of her sometimes, I have a further prospect. Sir Lionel's
25 daughters, which are in her charge, both like me, but the
youngest I pitch upon. And because I can't marry 'em

both, my young nobility, Mr Squab, shall have the other
sister. But I'll bubble him afterwards. Thus I'll raise my
fortune, which is all I want, for I am an agreeable man and
30   everybody likes me.
    Enter Boy.
BOY 'Tis Mr Squab, sir.
DAINTY Call him up, but comb your periwig first. Let me
comb it. You are the laziest sloven!

The Maimed Debauchee

As some brave admiral, in former war
Deprived of force but pressed with courage still,
Two rival fleets appearing from afar,
Crawls to the top of an adjacent hill,

5   From whence (with thoughts full of concern) he views
The wise and daring conduct of the fight,
And each bold action to his mind renews
His present glory and his past delight;

From his fierce eyes flashes of rage he throws,
10 As from black clouds when lightning breaks away,
Transported, thinks himself amidst his foes,
And absent, yet enjoys the bloody day;

So when my days of impotence approach,
And I'm by pox and wine's unlucky chance
15 Forced from the pleasing billows of debauch
On the dull shore of lazy temperance,

My pains at least some respite shall afford,
Whilst I behold the battles they maintain
When fleets of glasses sail about the board,
20 From whose broadsides volleys of wit shall rain;

Nor shall the sight of honourable scars,
Which my too forward valour did procure,
Frighten new-listed soldiers from the wars:
Past joys have more than paid what I endure.

25   Should any youth (worth being drunk) prove nice
And from his fair inviter meanly shrink,
'Twould please the ghost of my departed Vice
If at my counsel he repent and drink.

Or should some cold-complexioned sot forbid,
30   With his dull morals, our bold night alarms,
I'll fire his blood by telling what I did
When I was strong and able to bear arms.

I'll tell of whores attacked (their lords at home),
Bawds' quarters beaten up and fortress won,
35   Windows demolished, watches overcome,
And handsome ills by my contrivance done.

Nor shall our love-fits, Cloris, be forgot,
When each the well-looked linkboy strove t'enjoy,
And the best kiss was the deciding lot
40   Whether the boy fucked you, or I the boy.

With tales like these I will such heat inspire
As to important mischief shall incline;
I'll make him long some ancient church to fire
And fear no lewdness he's called to by wine.

45   Thus statesmanlike I'll saucily impose
And safe from action valiantly advise,
Sheltered in impotence urge you to blows,
And being good for nothing else, be wise.

A Very Heroical Epistle from My Lord All-Pride to Doll-Common

The Argument: *Doll-Common being forsaken by My Lord All-Pride and having written him a most lamentable Letter, his Lordship sends her the following Answer.*

Madam,
    If you're deceived, it is not by my cheat,
For all disguises are below the great.

What man or woman upon earth can say
I ever used 'em well above a day?
How is it then that I inconstant am?
He changes not who always is the same.
In my dear self I centre everything,
My servants, friends, my mistress, and my King,
Nay, heaven and earth to that one point I bring.
Well-mannered, honest, generous, and stout
(Names by dull fools to plague mankind found out),
Should I regard, I must myself constrain,
And 'tis my maxim to avoid all pain.
You fondly look for what none e'er could find,
Deceive yourself, and then call me unkind,
And by false reasons would my falsehood prove,
For 'tis as natural to change as love.
You may as justly at the sun repine
Because alike it does not always shine.
No glorious thing was ever made to stay;
My blazing star but visits and away,
As fatal too it shines as those i'th' skies;
'Tis never seen but some great lady dies.
The boasted favour you so precious hold
To me's no more than changing of my gold.
Whate'er you gave, I paid you back in bliss,
Then where's the obligation, pray, of this?
If heretofore you found grace in my eyes,
Be thankful for it and let that suffice.
But women, beggar-like, still haunt the door
Where they've received a charity before.
O happy sultan, whom we barbarous call,
How much refined art thou above us all!
Who envies not the joys of thy serail?
Thee, like some god, the trembling crowd adore,
Each man's thy slave and womankind thy whore.
Methinks I see thee underneath the shade
Of golden canopies supinely laid,
Thy crouching slaves all silent as the night,
But at thy nod all active as the light.

Secure in solid sloth thou there dost reign
And feel'st the joys of love without the pain.
Each female courts thee with a wishing eye,
While thou with awful pride walk'st careless by,
45   Till thy kind pledge at last marks out the dame
Thou fanciest most to quench thy present flame.
Then from thy bed submissive she retires
And thankful for thy grace no more requires.
No loud reproach nor fond unwelcome sound
50   Of women's tongues thy sacred ear dares wound.
If any do, a nimble mute straight ties
The true-love knot and stops her foolish cries.
Thou fear'st no injured kinsman's threatening blade
Nor midnight ambushes by rivals laid;
55   While here with aching hearts our joys we taste
Disturbed by swords like Damocles's feast.

*To all Gentlemen, Ladies, and Others, whether of City,
Town, or Country, Alexander Bendo wisheth all Health
and Prosperity*

Whereas this famous metropolis of England (and were the
endeavours of its worthy inhabitants equal to their power,
merit, and virtue, I should not stick to denounce it in a short
time the metropolis of the whole world), whereas, I say, this
5   city (as most great ones are) has ever been infested with a
numerous company of such whose arrogant confidence, backed
with their ignorance, has enabled them to impose upon the
people, either by premeditated cheats or at best the palpable,
dull, and empty mistakes of their self-deluded imaginations in
10   physic, chemical and Galenic, in astrology, physiognomy, palm-
istry, mathematics, alchemy, and even in government itself:
the last of which I will not propose to discourse of or meddle
at all in, since it no ways belongs to my trade or vocation, as
the rest do, which (thanks to my God) I find much more safe,
15   I think, equally honest, and therefore more profitable. But as
to all the former, they have been so erroneously practised by

many unlearned wretches whom poverty and neediness for the most part (if not the restless itch of deceiving) has forced to straggle and wander in unknown paths, that even the profes-
20 sions themselves, though originally the products of the most learned and wise men's laborious studies and experiences and by them left a wealthy and glorious inheritance for ages to come, seem by this bastard race of quacks and cheats to have been run out of all wisdom, learning, perspicuousness, and
25 truth with which they were so plentifully stocked and now run into a repute of mere mists, imaginations, errors, and deceits such as, in the management of these idle professors, indeed they were.

You will therefore (I hope) gentlemen, ladies, and others
30 deem it but just that I, who for some years have with all faithfulness and assiduity courted these arts and received such signal favours from them that have admitted me to the happy and full enjoyment of themselves and trusted me with their greatest secrets, should with an earnestness and concern more
35 than ordinary, take their parts against these impudent fops whose saucy, impertinent addresses and pretensions have brought such scandal upon their most immaculate honours and reputations.

Besides, I hope you will not think I could be so impudent
40 that, if I had intended any such foul play myself, I would have given you so fair warning by my severe observations upon others. *Qui alterum incusat probri, ipsum se intueri oportet.* PLAUTUS. However, Gentlemen, in a world like this, where virtue is so exactly counterfeited and hypocrisy so generally
45 taken notice of that everyone (armed with suspicion) stands upon his guard against it, 'twill be very hard, for a stranger especially, to escape censure. All I shall say for myself on this score is this: if I appear to anyone like a counterfeit, even for the sake of that chiefly ought I to be construed a true man.
50 Who is the counterfeit's example, his original, and that which he employs his industry and pains to imitate and copy? Is it therefore my fault if the cheat by his wits and endeavours makes himself so like me that consequently I cannot avoid resembling of him? Consider, pray, the valiant and the coward,
55 the wealthy merchant and the bankrupt, the politician and the

fool; they are the same in many things and differ but in one
alone. The valiant man holds up his head, looks confidently
round about him, wears a sword, courts a lord's wife and owns
it. So does the coward. One only point of honour, and that's
60   courage which like false metal one only trial can discover,
makes the distinction. The bankrupt walks the Exchange, buys
bargains, draws bills and accepts them with the richest whilst
paper and credit are current coin. That which makes the
difference is real cash, a great defect indeed, and yet but
65   one, and that the last found out, and still 'till then the least
perceived. Now for the politician. He is a grave, deliberating,
close, prying man. Pray, are there not grave, deliberating,
close, prying fools?

70   If then the difference betwixt all these (though infinite in
effect) be so nice in all appearance, will you expect it should be
otherwise betwixt the false physician, astrologer, &c. and the
true? The first calls himself learned doctor, sends forth his
bills, gives physic and counsel, tells and foretells. The other is
75   bound to do just as much. 'Tis only your experience must
distinguish betwixt them, to which I willingly submit myself.
I'll only say something to the honour of the mountebank, in
case you discover me to be one.

        Reflect a little what kind of creature 'tis. He is one then
80   who is fain to supply some higher ability he pretends to with
craft; he draws great companies to him by undertaking strange
things which can never be effected. The politician (by his
example no doubt) finding how the people are taken with
specious miraculous impossibilities, plays the same game, pro-
85   tests, declares, promises I know not what things which he is
sure can never be brought about. The people believe, are
deluded, and pleased. The expectation of a future good, which
shall never befall them, draws their eyes off a present evil.
Thus are *they* kept and established in subjection, peace, and
90   obedience, *he* in greatness, wealth, and power. So you see the
politician is and must be a mountebank in state affairs; and the
mountebank no doubt, if he thrives, is an arrant politician in
physic. But that I may not prove too tedious, I will proceed
faithfully to inform you what are the things in which I pretend
95   chiefly at this time to serve my country.

First, I will (by leave of God) perfectly cure that *labes Britannica* or grand English disease, the scurvy, and that with such ease to my patient that he shall not be sensible of the least inconvenience whilst I steal his distemper from him. I know there are many who treat this disease with mercury, antimony, and salts, being dangerous remedies in which I shall meddle very little and with great caution, but, by more secure, gentle, and less fallible medicines together with the observation of some few rules in diet, perfectly cure the patient, having freed him from all the symptoms, as looseness of the teeth, scorbutic spots, want of appetite, pains and lassitude in the limbs and joints, especially the legs. And to say true, there are few distempers in this nation that are not, or at least proceed not originally from, the scurvy, which were it well rooted out (as I make no question to do it from all those who shall come into my hands), there would not be heard of so many gouts, aches, dropsies, and consumptions; nay, even those thick and slimy humours which generate stones in the kidneys and bladder are for the most part offsprings of the scurvy. It would prove tedious to set down all its malignant race, but those who address themselves here shall be still informed by me of the nature of their distempers and the grounds I proceed upon to their cure. So will all reasonable people be satisfied that I treat them with care, honesty, and understanding, for I am not of their opinion who endeavour to render their vocations rather mysterious than useful and satisfactory.

I will not here make a catalogue of diseases and distempers. It behooves a physician, I am sure, to understand them all, but if any one come to me (as I think there are very few that have escaped my practice), I shall not be ashamed to own to my patient where I find myself to seek and at least he shall be secure with me from having experiments tried upon him, a privilege he can never hope to enjoy, either in the hands of the grand doctors of the court and town or in those of the lesser quacks and mountebanks.

It is thought fit that I assure you of great secrecy as well as care in diseases where it is requisite, whether venereal or other, as some peculiar to women, the green-sickness, weaknesses,

inflammations or obstructions in the stomach, reins, liver,
135   spleen, &c., for I would put no word in my bill that bears any
unclean sound; it is enough that I make myself understood. I
have seen physician's bills as bawdy as Aretine's *Dialogues*,
which no man that walks warily before God can approve of.
But I cure all suffocations in those parts producing fits of the
140   mother, convulsions, nocturnal inquietudes, and other strange
accidents not fit to be set down here, persuading young women
very often that their hearts are like to break for love, when God
knows the distemper lies far enough from that place.

I have likewise got the knowledge of a great secret to
145   cure barrenness (proceeding from any accidental cause, as it
often falls out, and no natural defect, for nature is easily
assisted, difficultly restored, but impossible to be made more
perfect by man than God himself had at first created and
bestowed it), which I have made use of for many years with
150   great success, especially this last year wherein I have cured one
woman that had been married twenty years, and another that
had been married one and twenty years, and two women that
had been three times married, as I can make appear by the
testimony of several persons in London, Westminster, and
155   other places thereabouts. The medicines I use cleanse and
strengthen the womb and are all to be taken in the space of
seven days. And because I do not intend to deceive any
person, upon discourse with them I will tell them whether I
am like to do them any good. My usual contract is to receive
160   one half of what is agreed upon when the party shall be quick
with child, the other half when she is brought to bed.

Cures of this kind I have done signal and many, for the
which I doubt not but I have the good wishes and hearty
prayer of many families who had else pined out their days
165   under the deplorable and reproachful misfortunes of barren
wombs, leaving plentiful estates and possessions to be inherited
by strangers.

As to astrological predictions, physiognomy, divination by
dreams and otherwise (palmistry I have no faith in because
170   there can be no reason alleged for it), my own experience has
convinced me more of their considerable effects and marvellous

operations, chiefly in the directions of future proceedings to the avoiding of dangers that threaten and laying hold of advantages that might offer themselves.

175   I say, my own practice has convinced me more than all the sage and wise writings extant of these matters. For I might say this for myself (did it not look like ostentation) that I have very seldom failed in my predictions and often been very serviceable in my advice. How far I am capable in this way, I
180   am sure is not fit to be delivered in print. Those who have no opinion of the truth of this art will not, I suppose, come to me about it; such as have, I make no question of giving them ample satisfaction.

Nor will I be ashamed to set down here my willingness to
185   practise rare secrets (though somewhat collateral to my profession) for the help, conservation, and augmentation of beauty and comeliness, a thing created at first by God chiefly for the glory of his own name and then for the better establishment of mutual love between man and woman. For when God had
190   bestowed on man the power of strength and wisdom and thereby rendered woman liable to the subjection of his absolute will, it seemed but requisite that she should be endued likewise, in recompense, with some quality that might beget in him admiration of her and so enforce his tenderness and love.

195   The knowledge of these secrets I gathered in my travels abroad (where I have spent my time ever since I was fifteen years old to this my nine and twentieth year) in France and Italy. Those that have travelled in Italy will tell you to what a miracle art does there assist nature in the preservation of
200   beauty, how women of forty bear the same countenance with those of fifteen, that ages are no ways distinguished by faces. Whereas here in England, look a horse in the mouth and a woman in the face, you presently know both their ages to a year. I will therefore give you such remedies that without
205   destroying your complexion (as most of your paints and daubings do) shall render them purely fair, clearing and preserving them from all spots, freckles, heats, pimples, and marks of the smallpox, or any other accidental ones, so the face be not seamed or scarred.

210   I will also cleanse and preserve your teeth white and round

as pearls, fastening them that are loose. Your gums shall be kept entire, as red as coral, your lips of the same colour and soft as you could wish your lawful kisses.

I will likewise administer that which shall cure the worst of
215 breaths, provided the lungs be not totally perished and impost-humated, as also certain and infallible remedies for those whose breaths are yet untainted, so that nothing but either a very long sickness or old age itself shall ever be able to spoil them.

220 I will besides (if it be desired) take away from their fatness who have overmuch, and add flesh to those that want it, without the least detriment to the constitution.

Now should Galen himself look out of his grave and tell me these were baubles below the profession of a physician, I
225 would boldly answer him that I take more glory in preserving God's image in its unblemished beauty upon one good face than I should do in patching up all the decayed carcasses in the world.

They that will do me the favour to come to me shall be
230 sure from three of the clock in the afternoon till eight at night at my lodgings in Tower street, next door to the sign of the Black Swan at a goldsmith's house, to find

Their humble servant,
Alexander Bendo.

An Allusion to Horace. The 10th Satire of the 1st Book

Nempe incomposito Dixi pede &c.

Well sir, 'tis granted I said Dryden's rhymes
Were stol'n, unequal, nay dull many times.
What foolish patron is there found of his
So blindly partial to deny me this?
5 But that his plays, embroidered up and down
With wit and learning, justly pleased the town
In the same paper I as freely own.
Yet having this allowed, the heavy mass
That stuffs up his loose volumes must not pass:

10 For by that rule I might as well admit
Crowne's tedious scenes for poetry and wit.
'Tis therefore not enough when your false sense
Hits the false judgement of an audience
Of clapping fools, assembling a vast crowd
15 Till the thronged playhouse crack with the dull load;
Though ev'n that talent merits in some sort
That can divert the rabble and the court,
Which blundering Settle never could attain,
And puzzling Otway labours at in vain.
20 But within due proportions circumscribe
Whate'er you write, that with a flowing tide
The style may rise, yet in its rise forbear
With useless words t'oppress the wearied ear.
Here be your language lofty, there more light,
25 Your rhetoric with your poetry unite.
For elegance' sake sometimes allay the force
Of epithets; 'twill soften the discourse.
A jest in scorn points out and hits the thing
More home than the morosest satire's sting.
30 Shakespeare and Jonson did herein excel
And might in this be imitated well;
Whom refined Etherege copies not at all,
But is himself a sheer original;
Nor that slow drudge in swift Pindaric strains,
35 Flatman, who Cowley imitates with pains,
And rides a jaded muse, whipped with loose reins.
When Lee makes temperate Scipio fret and rave,
And Hannibal a whining amorous slave,
I laugh and wish the hot-brained fustian fool
40 In Busby's hands to be well lashed at school.
Of all our modern wits, none seems to me
Once to have touched upon true comedy
But hasty Shadwell and slow Wycherley.
Shadwell's unfinished works do yet impart
45 Great proofs of force of nature, none of art;
With just, bold strokes he dashes here and there,
Showing great mastery with little care,

And scorns to varnish his good touches o'er
To make the fools and women praise 'em more.
50 But Wycherley earns hard whate'er he gains;
He wants no judgement, nor he spares no pains.
He frequently excels, and at the least
Makes fewer faults than any of the best.
Waller, by nature for the bays designed,
55 With force and fire and fancy unconfined,
In panegyrics does excel mankind.
He best can turn, enforce, and soften things
To praise great conquerors or to flatter kings.
    For pointed satires I would Buckhurst choose,
60 The best good man with the worst-natured muse,
For songs and verses mannerly obscene,
That can stir nature up by springs unseen,
And without forcing blushes, warm the Queen.
    Sedley has that prevailing, gentle art,
65 That can with a resistless charm impart
The loosest wishes to the chastest heart,
Raise such a conflict, kindle such a fire,
Betwixt declining virtue and desire,
Till the poor vanquished maid dissolves away
70 In dreams all night, in sighs and tears all day.
    Dryden in vain tried this nice way of wit,
For he to be a tearing blade thought fit.
But when he would be sharp, he still was blunt;
To frisk his frolic fancy, he'd cry, 'Cunt',
75 Would give the ladies a dry bawdy bob,
And thus he got the name of Poet Squab.
But, to be just, 'twill to his praise be found
His excellencies more than faults abound;
Nor dare I from his sacred temples tear
80 That laurel which he best deserves to wear.
But does not Dryden find ev'n Jonson dull;
Fletcher and Beaumont uncorrect and full
Of lewd lines, as he calls 'em; Shakespeare's style
Stiff and affected; to his own the while
85 Allowing all the justness that his pride
So arrogantly had to these denied?

And may not I have leave impartially
To search and censure Dryden's works and try
If those gross faults his choice pen does commit
90   Proceed from want of judgement or of wit;
Or if his lumpish fancy does refuse
Spirit and grace to his loose slattern muse?
Five hundred verses every morning writ
Proves you no more a poet than a wit.
95   Such scribbling authors have been seen before;
Mustapha, *The English Princess*, forty more
Were things perhaps composed in half an hour.
To write what may securely stand the test
Of being well read over, thrice at least,
100   Compare each phrase, examine every line,
Weigh every word, and every thought refine,
Scorn all applause the vile rout can bestow
And be content to please those few who know.
Canst thou be such a vain, mistaken thing
105   To wish thy works might make a playhouse ring
With the unthinking laughter and poor praise
Of fops and ladies, factious for thy plays?
Then send a cunning friend to learn thy doom
From the shrewd judges of the drawing room.
110   I've no ambition on that idle score,
But say with Betty Morris heretofore
When a court lady called her Buckhurst's whore,
'I please one man of wit, am proud on't too;
Let all the coxcombs dance to bed to you.'
115   Should I be troubled when the purblind knight,
Who squints more in his judgement than his sight,
Picks silly faults, and censures what I write;
Or when the poor-fed poets of the town
For scraps and coach-room cry my verses down?
120   I loathe the rabble, 'tis enough for me
If Sedley, Shadwell, Sheppard, Wycherley,
Godolphin, Butler, Buckhurst, Buckingham,
And some few more, whom I omit to name,
Approve my sense: I count their censure fame.

[*Leave this gaudy, gilded stage*]

Leave this gaudy, gilded stage,
From custom more than use frequented,
Where fools of either sex and age
Crowd to see themselves presented.
5   To love's theatre, the bed,
Youth and beauty fly together
And act so well it may be said
The laurel there was due to either.
'Twixt strifes of love and war the difference lies in this:
10 When neither overcomes, love's triumph greater is.

Against Constancy

Tell me no more of constancy,
    The frivolous pretense
Of cold age, narrow jealousy,
    Disease, and want of sense.

5 Let duller fools on whom kind chance
    Some easy heart has thrown,
Despairing higher to advance,
    Be kind to one alone.

Old men and weak, whose idle flame
10   Their own defects discovers,
Since changing can but spread their shame,
    Ought to be constant lovers,

But we, whose hearts do justly swell
    With no vainglorious pride,
15 Who know how we in love excel,
    Long to be often tried.

Then bring my bath and strew my bed,
    As each kind night returns:
I'll change a mistress till I'm dead,
20   And fate change me for worms.

To the Postboy

ROCHESTER   Son of a whore, God damn you, can you tell
             A peerless peer the readiest way to Hell?
             I've outswilled Bacchus, sworn of my own make
             Oaths would fright Furies and make Pluto quake.
5   I've swived more whores more ways than Sodom's walls
             E'er knew, or the college of Rome's cardinals.
             Witness heroic scars, look here, ne'er go,
             Cerecloths and ulcers from top to toe.
             Frighted at my own mischiefs I have fled
10   And bravely left my life's defender dead,
             Broke houses to break chastity, and dyed
             That floor with murder which my lust denied.
             Pox on't, why do I speak of these poor things?
             I have blasphemed my God and libelled kings.
15   The readiest way to Hell? Come quick, ne'er stir.
        BOY The readiest way, my lord, 's by Rochester.

[*God bless our good and gracious King*]

God bless our good and gracious King,
    Whose promise none relies on,
Who never said a foolish thing,
    Nor ever did a wise one.

Love and Life

All my past life is mine no more;
    The flying hours are gone
Like transitory dreams given o'er,
Whose images are kept in store
5   By memory alone.

Whatever is to come is not;
 How can it then be mine?
The present moment's all my lot
And that, as fast as it is got,
10 Phillis, is wholly thine.

Then talk not of inconstancy,
 False hearts, and broken vows,
If I by miracle can be
This livelong minute true to thee,
15 'Tis all that heaven allows.

The Epilogue to Circe

Some few from wit have this true maxim got
That 'tis still better to be pleased than not
And therefore never their own torment plot,
While the malicious critics still agree
5 To loathe each play they come and pay to see;
The first know 'tis a meaner part of sense
To find a fault than taste an excellence,
Therefore they praise and strive to like, while these
Are dully vain of being hard to please.
10 Poets and women have an equal right
To hate the dull, who dead to all delight
Feel pain alone and have no joy but spite.
'Twas impotence did first this vice begin,
Fools censure wit as old men rail of sin,
15 Who envy pleasure which they cannot taste,
And good for nothing would be wise at last.
Since therefore to the women it appears
That all these enemies of wit are theirs,
Our poet the dull herd no longer fears.
20 Whate'er his fate may prove, 'twill be his pride
To stand or fall with beauty on his side.

On Mistress Willis

Against the charms our ballocks have,
    How weak all human skill is,
Since they can make a man a slave
    To such a bitch as Willis.

5   Whom that I may describe throughout,
    Assist me, bawdy powers;
I'll write upon a double clout
    And dip my pen in flowers.

Her look's demurely impudent,
10   Ungainly beautiful,
Her modesty is insolent,
    Her mirth is pert and dull.

A prostitute to all the town
    And yet with no man friends,
15 She rails and scolds when she lies down
    And curses when she spends.

Bawdy in thoughts, precise in words,
    Ill-natured though a whore,
Her belly is a bag of turds,
20   And her cunt a common shore.

Song

By all love's soft yet mighty powers,
    It is a thing unfit
That men should fuck in time of flowers
    Or when the smock's beshit.

5   Fair nasty nymph, be clean and kind
    And all my joys restore
By using paper still behind
    And sponges for before.

My spotless flames can ne'er decay
10   If after every close
My smoking prick escape the fray
   Without a bloody nose.

If thou wouldst have me true, be wise
   And take to cleanly sinning;
15 None but fresh lovers' pricks can rise
   At Phillis in foul linen.

Upon Nothing

Nothing, thou elder brother even to Shade,
Thou hadst a being ere the world was made,
And (well fixed) art alone of ending not afraid.

Ere time and place were, Time and Place were not,
5 When primitive Nothing, Something straight begot;
Then all proceeded from the great united what.

Something, the general attribute of all,
Severed from thee, its sole original,
Into thy boundless self must undistinguished fall.

10 Yet Something did thy mighty power command
And from thy fruitful Emptiness's hand
Snatched men, beasts, birds, fire, water, air, and land.

Matter, the wicked'st offspring of thy race,
By Form assisted, flew from thy embrace,
15 And rebel Light obscured thy reverend dusky face.

With Form and Matter, Time and Place did join;
Body, thy foe, with these did leagues combine
To spoil thy peaceful reign and ruin all thy line.

But turncoat Time assists the foe in vain
20 And bribed by thee destroys their short-lived reign
And to thy hungry womb drives back the slaves again.

Thy mysteries are hid from laic eyes,
And the divine alone by warrant pries
Into thy bosom, where the truth in private lies.

25 Yet this of thee the wise may truly say,
Thou from the virtuous nothing tak'st away,
And to be part of thee the wicked wisely pray.

Great Negative, how vainly would the wise
Inquire, define, distinguish, teach, devise
30 Didst thou not stand to point their dull philosophies.

Is or Is Not, the two great ends of Fate,
And True or False, the subject of debate
That perfects or destroys the vast designs of state,

When they have racked the politician's breast,
35 Within thy bosom most securely rest
And when reduced to thee are least unsafe and best.

But Nothing, why does Something still permit
That sacred monarchs should at council sit
With persons thought, at best, for nothing fit,

40 While weighty Something modestly abstains
From princes' coffers and from statesman's brains;
And nothing there like stately Nothing reigns.

Nothing, that dwells with fools in grave disguise,
For whom they reverend forms and shapes devise,
45 Lawn sleeves, and furs, and gowns, when they like thee look
    wise.

French truth, Dutch prowess, British policy,
Hibernian learning, Scotch civility,
Spaniards' dispatch, Danes' wit are mainly seen in thee.

The great man's gratitude to his best friend,
50 Kings' promises, whores' vows, to thee they bend,
Flow swiftly into thee and in thee ever end.

The Earl of Rochester's Answer to a Paper of Verses
sent him by L[ady] B[etty] Felton and taken out of the
Translation of Ovid's Epistles, *1680*

What strange surprise to meet such words as these,
Such terms of horror were ne'er chose to please,
To meet, midst pleasures of a jovial night,
Words that can only give amaze and fright,
5 No gentler thought that does to love invite.
Were it not better far your arms t'employ
Grasping a lover in pursuit of joy
Than handling sword and pen, weapons unfit?
Your sex gains conquest by their charms and wit.
10 Of writers slain I could with pleasure hear,
Approve of fights, o'erjoyed to cause a tear;
So slain, I mean, that she should soon revive,
Pleased in my arms to find herself alive.

Abbreviations and Short Titles of Works Frequently Cited

AND	B. E., *A New Dictionary of the Terms Ancient and Modern of the Canting Crew . . .* (1699).
Aubrey 1898	John Aubrey, *Brief Lives*, ed. Andrew Clark, 2 vols. (1898).
Barton	See Righter.
BDAA	*A Biographical Dictionary of Actors, Actresses . . .*, ed. Philip H. Highfill, Jr., *et al.*, 12 vols. to date, Illinois University Press (1973–).
Beaumont and Fletcher	*The Works of Francis Beaumont and John Fletcher*, ed. Arnold Glover, 10 vols. (1905–12).
Biographia Britannica 1747–66	*Biographia Britannica: or, The Lives of the Most Eminent Persons*, ed. William Oldys *et al.*, 6 vols. in 7 (1747–66).
B.L.	The British Library, London.
Blake 1957	*The Complete Writings of William Blake*, ed. Geoffrey Keynes (1957).
Blount 1680	Charles Blount, *The Two First Books of Philostratus, concerning the Life of Apollonius Tyaneus* (1680).
Bodl.	The Bodleian Library, Oxford.
Burnet 1680	Gilbert Burnet, *Some Passages of the Life and Death of the Right Honourable John Earl of Rochester* (1680).
Butler 1928	Samuel Butler, *Satires and Miscellaneous Poetry and Prose*, ed. René Lamar (1928).
Butler 1967	Samuel Butler, *Hudibras*, ed. John Wilders (1967).
Congreve 1967	*The Complete Plays of William Congreve*, ed. Herbert Davis (1967).

Cowley 1905	Abraham Cowley, *Poems*, ed. A. R. Waller (1905).
Crocker 1937	S. F. Crocker, *West Virginia University Studies*, III. *Philological Papers* 2 (May 1937), 57–73.
Culpeper 1652	Nicholas Culpeper, *The English Physician: Or, An Astrologo-Physical Discourse of the Vulgar Herbs of this Nation* ... (1652).
Davies 1969	Paul C. Davies, *Comparative Literature* 21 (1969), 348–55.
Dennis 1939–43	*The Critical Works of John Dennis*, ed. Edward N. Hooker, 2 vols. (1939–43).
DNB	*The Dictionary of National Biography*, ed. Sir Leslie Stephen and Sir Sidney Lee, 22 vols. (1949–50).
Donne 1912	*The Poems of John Donne*, ed. Herbert J. C. Grierson, 2 vols. (1912).
Dorset 1979	*The Poems of Charles Sackville, Sixth Earl of Dorset*, ed. Brice Harris (1979).
Downes 1987	John Downes, *Roscius Anglicanus* [*1708*], ed. Judith Milhous and Robert D. Hume (1987).
Dryden 1882–93	*The Works of John Dryden*, ed. Sir Walter Scott and George Saintsbury, 18 vols. (1882–93).
Dryden 1956–	*The Works of John Dryden*, ed. Edward N. Hooker, H. T. Swedenberg *et al.* (1956–).
Eachard 1672	[John Eachard], *Mr Hobb's State of Nature Considered; in a Dialogue between Philautus and Timothy*, 2nd ed. (1672).
ECS	*Eighteenth-Century Studies*, 1967– .
Ellis 1951	Frank H. Ellis, *PMLA* 66 (1951), 971–1008.
ELN	*English Language Notes*, 1962– .
Essex Papers 1890	*Essex Papers. Volume I. 1672–1679*, ed. Osmund Airy (1890).
Etherege 1963	*The Poems of Sir George Etherege*, ed. James Thorpe (1963).

Farley-Hills 1978 — David Farley-Hills, *Rochester's Poetry* (1978).

Griffin 1973 — Dustin H. Griffin, *Satires against Man. The Poems of Rochester* (1973).

Halifax 1912 — *The Complete Works of George Savile First Marquess of Halifax*, ed. Walter Raleigh (1912).

Hamilton 1930 — Anthony Hamilton, *Memoirs of the Comte de Gramont*, tr. Peter Quennell (1930).

Hearne 1884–1918 — *Remarks and Collections of Thomas Hearne*, ed. C. E. Doble, 11 vols. (1884–1918).

HMC *Rutland MSS*. — *Twelfth Report, Appendix, Part IV, The Manuscripts of His Grace the Duke of Rutland, G.C.B., Preserved at Belvoir Castle*, 4 vols. (1888–1905).

HMC *Seventh Report* — *Seventh Report of the Royal Commission on Historical Manuscripts*, Part I. Appendix (1879).

Hobbes 1935 — Thomas Hobbes, *The Leviathan, or The Matter, Forme & Power of a Commonwealth, Ecclesiasticall and Civill*, ed. A. R. Waller (1935).

Hutton 1989 — Ronald Hutton, *Charles the Second, King of England, Scotland, and Ireland* (1989).

I Modi 1988 — *I Modi, The Sixteen Pleasures . . . Giulio Romano, Marcantonio Raimondi, Pietro Aretino, and Count Jean-Frédéric-Maximilien de Waldeck*, ed. Lynne Lawner (1988).

Johnson 1755 — *A Dictionary of the English Language*, ed. Samuel Johnson, 2 vols. (1755).

Johnson 1779–81 — Samuel Johnson, *Prefaces, Biographical and Critical, to the Works of the English Poets*, 10 vols. (1779–81).

Jonson 1925–52 — *Ben Jonson*, ed. C. H. Herford *et al.*, 11 vols. (1925–52).

Langbaine 1691 — Gerard Langbaine, *An Account of the English Dramatick Poets* (1691).

Lee 1954 — *The Works of Nathaniel Lee*, ed. Thomas B. Stroup *et al.*, 2 vols. (1954).

Leneve 1873	Peter Leneve, *Leneve's Pedigrees of the Knights*, ed. George W. Marshall (1873).
London Stage	*The London Stage 1660–1800*, ed. William Van Lennep *et al.*, 5 vols. in 11 (1960–68).
Love 1972	Harold Love, in *Restoration Literature. Critical Approaches* (1972).
Love 1981	Harold Love, in *Poetry and Drama 1570–1700*, ed. Antony Coleman *et al.* (1981).
Machiavelli 1977	Niccolò Machiavelli, *Il Principe* (1532), tr. Robert M. Adams (1977).
Manning 1986	Gillian Manning, *N&Q* 231 (1986), 38–40.
Marvell 1927	*The Poems and Letters of Andrew Marvell*, ed. H. M. Margoliouth, 2 vols. (1927).
Milton 1931–8	*The Works of John Milton*, ed. Frank A. Patterson *et al.*, 18 vols. in 20 (1931–8).
MLR	*Modern Language Review*, 1905– .
Montaigne 1700	*Essays of Michael Seigneur de Montaigne*, tr. Charles Cotton, 3 vols. (1700).
Moskovit 1968	Leonard A. Moskovit, *SEL* 8 (1968), 451–3.
Motif-Index	*Motif-Index of Folk-Literature*, ed. Stith Thompson, 2nd ed., 6 vols. (1955). Folklore motifs are cited by the letter-and-number system of this work.
N&Q	*Notes and Queries; for Readers and Writers*, 1849– .
OED	*The Oxford English Dictionary*, ed. James A. H. Murray *et al.*, 2nd ed., 20 vols. (1989).
Oldham 1987	*The Poems of John Oldham*, ed. Harold F. Brooks *et al.* (1987).
Parsons 1680	Robert Parsons, *A Sermon Preached at the Funeral of the Rt Honorable John Earl of Rochester* (1680).
Paulson 1972	Kristoffer F. Paulson, *Satire Newsletter* 10 (1972), 28–9.
Pepys	*The Diary of Samuel Pepys*, ed. Robert Latham *et al.*, 11 vols. (1970–83).
Pinto 1935	Vivian de S. Pinto, *Rochester: Portrait of a Restoration Poet* (1935, rptd. 1971).
Pinto 1962	Vivian de S. Pinto, *Enthusiast in Wit. A*

	Portrait of John Wilmot Earl of Rochester 1647–1680 (1962).
POAS, Yale	*Poems on Affairs of State*, ed. George deF. Lord *et al.*, 7 vols (1963–75).
Pope 1939–67	*The Twickenham Edition of the Poems of Alexander Pope*, ed. John Butt *et al.*, 10 vols. in 11 (1939–67).
Pound 1934	Ezra Pound, *ABC of Reading* (1934).
PQ	*Philological Quarterly*, 1922– .
Reliquiae Hearnianae	Thomas Hearne, *Reliquiae Hearnianae*, ed. Philip Bliss, 2nd ed., 3 vols. (1869).
RES	*Review of English Studies*, 1925–50, n.s., 1950– .
Righter 1968	Anne Righter, Chatterton Lecture, *Proceedings of the British Academy* 53 (1968), 47–69.
Rochester 1680	*Poems on Several Occasions by the Right Honourable, the E. of R—* (1680). Rochester 1680 falls into three parts: 1680[1] (pp. 3–54) includes 15 satires and translations of which 11 are Rochester's; 1680[2] (pp. 54–75) includes 23 songs of which 20 are Rochester's; 1680[3] (pp. 76–151) includes 34 poems of which 6 are Rochester's (Vieth 1963, 93–100).
Rochester 1685	*Poems on Several Occasions, Written by a late Person of Honour*, London: for A. Thorncome (1685). The Thorncome edition of Rochester 1680 adds five new poems, two by Thomas Randolph and three included in the present volume.
Rochester 1691	*Poems on Several Occasions: with Valentinian, A Tragedy. Written by the Right Honourable John Late Earl of Rochester* [ed. Thomas Rymer], London: for Jacob Tonson (1691).
Rochester 1707 (Bragge)	*The Miscellaneous Works of the Right Honourable the late Earls of Rochester and Roscommon. With the Memoirs of the Life and Character of the late Earl of Rochester, in a*

Letter to the Dutchess of Mazarine. By Mons. St. Evremont, London: sold by B. Bragge (1691) (Case 242). This is the first edition to include the memoir of Rochester by Pseudo-St Evremond.

Rochester 1926	*Collected Works of John Wilmot Earl of Rochester*, ed. John Hayward, London: Nonesuch (1926).
Rochester 1953	*Poems by John Wilmot Earl of Rochester*, ed. Vivian de S. Pinto (1953, 2nd ed. 1964).
Rochester 1968	*The Complete Poems of John Wilmot, Earl of Rochester*, ed. David M. Vieth (1968).
Rochester 1980	*Rochester Selected Satires and Other Poems*, ed. David Brooks (1980).
Rochester 1984	*The Poems of John Wilmot Earl of Rochester*, ed. Keith Walker (1984).
Rochester *Letters* 1980	*The Letters of John Wilmot Earl of Rochester*, ed. Jeremy Treglown (1980).
Rowzee 1671	Lodwick Rowzee, *The Queens Wells. That is, A Treatise of the nature and vertues of the Tunbridge Water* (1671, 1st ed. 1632).
Savile Correspondence	*Savile Correspondence. Letters to and from Henry Savile, Esq., Envoy at Paris, and Vice-Chamberlain to Charles II and James II*, ed. William D. Cooper (1858).
SEL	*Studies in English Literature 1500–1900*, 1960– .
Shadwell 1927	*The Complete Works of Thomas Shadwell*, ed. Montagu Summers, 5 vols. (1927).
Simpson 1966	Claude M. Simpson, *The British Broadside Ballad and its Music* (1966).
Sitter 1976	John E. Sitter, *PLL* 12 (1976), 285–98.
Spence 1966	Joseph Spence, *Observations, Anecdotes, and Characters of Books and Men Collected from Conversation*, ed. James M. Osborn, 2 vols. (1966).
Sterne 1928	Laurence Sterne, *A Sentimental Journey through France and Italy* (1928).
Sterne 1940	Laurence Sterne, *The Life and Opinions of*

	Tristram Shandy, Gentleman, ed. James A. Work (1940).
Stillingfleet 1675	Edward Stillingfleet, *A Sermon Preach'd before the King Feb. 24, 1674/5* (1675).
Suckling 1971	*The Works of Sir John Suckling*, ed. Thomas Clayton *et al.*, 2 vols. (1971).
Swift 1937	*The Poems of Jonathan Swift*, ed. Harold Williams, 1 vol. in 3 (1937).
Swift 1939–68	*The Prose Writings of Jonathan Swift*, ed. Herbert Davis *et al.*, 14 vols. (1939–68).
T.C.	*The Term Catalogues 1668–1709 A.D.*, ed. Edward Arber, 3 vols. (1903).
Thormählen 1988	Marianne Thormählen, *English Studies* 69 (1988), 396–409.
Tibullus 1971	*Albii Tibulli Aliorumque Carminum Libri Tres*, ed. Fridericus W. Lenz *et al.* (1971).
Tilley	Morris P. Tilley, *A Dictionary of the Proverbs in England in the Sixteenth and Seventeenth Centuries* (1950).
TLS	*[The London] Times Literary Supplement*, 1902– .
Treglown 1973	Jeremy Treglown, *RES* n.s. 24 (1973), 42–8.
Treglown 1976	Jeremy Treglown, *N&Q* 221 (1976), 554–9.
Treglown 1980	Jeremy Treglown, *MLR* 75 (1980), 18–47.
Treglown 1982	*Spirit of Wit: Reconsiderations of Rochester*, ed. Jeremy Treglown (1982).
Vieth 1963	David M. Vieth, *Attribution in Restoration Poetry* (1963).
Vieth and Griffin 1988	David M. Vieth and Dustin Griffin, *Rochester and Court Poetry* (1988).
Waller 1893	*The Poems of Edmund Waller*, ed. G. Thorn Drury (1893).
Wilcoxon 1979	Reba Wilcoxon, *Studies in Eighteenth-Century Culture* 8 (1979), 137–49.
Wilson 1976	John H. Wilson, *Court Satires of the Restoration* (1976).
Wing	*Short Title Catalogue of Books Printed in England, Scotland, Ireland, Wales, and*

British America . . . 1641–1700, ed. Donald Wing, 2nd ed., 3 vols. (1972–88).

Winn 1987   James A. Winn, *John Dryden and His World* (1987).

Wood 1813–20   Anthony à Wood, *Athenae Oxoniensis. An Exact History of all the Writers and Bishops who have had their Education in the University of Oxford*, 3rd ed., ed. Philip Bliss, 4 vols. (1813–20, rptd. 1967).

Wycherley 1979   *The Plays of William Wycherley*, ed. Arthur Friedman (1979).

Glossary

Unless otherwise stated the definitions are adapted from the second edition of the *Oxford English Dictionary* (1989).

alarm: a call to arms, a signal calling upon men to arm.

alcove: a vaulted recess in which is placed a bed of state: 'in the close Alcove, /. . . *Keppell* and He are *Ganymede* and *Jove*' (*POAS*, Yale, VI 18).

antic: absurd from fantastic incongruity, grotesque, bizarre, uncouthly ludicrous.

arrant: a variant of 'errant', 'wandering, vagrant, vagabond', which from its frequent use in such expressions as *arrant thief*, became an intensive, 'thorough, notorious, downright'.

aspiring: desirous or advancement, ambitious.

balk: to pass over, overlook, refrain from noticing.

band: a falling collar, a pair of strips hanging down in front as part of a conventional dress, clerical, legal, or academic, resembling those worn by the Swiss Calvinist clergy.

bay: usually in plural: leaves or sprigs of bay-tree or laurel woven into a wreath or garland to reward a poet.

Bedlam: the Hospital of St Mary of Bethlehem, used as an asylum for mentally deranged persons; originally situated in Bishopsgate, in 1676 rebuilt near London Wall.

beer-glass: a glass holding half a pint.

before: in time previous to a time in question; already.

bend: bow in submission or reverence.

birthday coat: worn on the king's birthday.

blade: a gallant, attentive to women.

blot: a disgrace, fault, blemish.

board: a table (*obsolete*).

broke: penniless.

bubble: one that is cheated (*AND*).

buggery: sexual intercourse of men with one another.

bulk: a framework projecting from the front of a shop.

cadet: a younger son or brother, traditionally impoverished.

carman: a carter, carrier.

cerecloth: cloth impregnated with wax, used as a plaster in surgery in the treatment of venereal disease; cf. Sir Carr Scrope is 'lapt in sear cloth'; Sir Alexander Fraser 'may cure his pox' (HMC *Rutland* MSS., II 37; Wilson 1976, 240).

chaffer: bargain, haggle about terms or price.

challenge: assert one's title to, lay claim to, demand as a right (*obsolete*).

charming: exercising magic power.

City: that part of London situated within the ancient boundaries which is under the jurisdiction of the Lord Mayor and Corporation; more particularly, the business part of this, in the neighbourhood of the Royal Exchange, the centre of financial and commercial activity.

civility: freedom from barbarity; the state of being civilized (Johnson 1755).

clip: clasp with the arms, embrace, hug.

close: sexual encounter.

clout: a piece of cloth, especially a small or worthless piece or one put to mean uses; slang for what is now called a sanitary towel (Rochester 1980, 110).

clown: a countryman; one very ill-bred or unmannerly (*AND*).

coast: quarter, part (*obsolete*).

cob: leader.

cokes: a silly fellow, simpleton, one easily taken in. Bartholomew Cokes is the comic victim in Ben Jonson's *Bartholomew Fair* (1614).

colour: outward appearance, show.

combine: band together, confederate, or league.

comfortable: cf. 'importance'.

common: free to be used by everyone; low-class, vulgar, unrefined.

complexioned: having a specified mental constitution, disposition, or temperament (*obsolete*).

conceited: having an overweening opinion of oneself (*OED*); wise in his own opinion (*AND*).

conventicle: a meeting of nonconformists, or dissenters from the

Church of England, for religious worship during the period when such meetings were prohibited by law.

cony: a rabbit.

coxcomb: a fool, simpleton (*obsolete*).

creature: a human being, a term of reprobation or contempt; cf. 'a thing' (20.89).

cully: a fool or silly creature that is easily drawn in and cheated by whores or rogues (*AND*).

dainty: possessing delicate taste, fastidious; valuable, fine, choice, excellent.

dazzled: having lost the faculty of distinct and steady vision, especially from gazing at too bright light.

diet: take one's ordinary meals.

Dingboy: a rogue, hector, bully, sharper (*AND*).

discreetly: with self-regarding prudence.

do the trick: accomplish one's purpose, do what is wanted.

drawing room: shortened from withdrawing-room, a private chamber attached to a more public room.

drudge: toil at laborious and distasteful work.

dry: feeling no emotion.

dry-bob: coition without ejaculation (Partridge 1951).

elf: in a depreciatory sense, 'a poor creature'.

engine: a mechanical contrivance, machine.

errant: straying from the proper course.

experience: experiments (*obsolete*).

expire: to have an orgasm.

fantastic: having a lively imagination; fanciful, impulsive, capricious.

fiddle: one to whose music others dance; hence, a mirth-maker, jester.

fill out: pour out.

first rate: of the first rate (said of vessels, especially of the old three-deckers carrying 74–120 guns, such as *The Triumph* on which Rochester served in the second Dutch War); hence of the highest class or degree of excellence.

flowers: menstrual discharge.

fold: posture adopted during sexual intercourse.

fond: having strong affection for; eager, desirous.

fop: a fool (*obsolete*).

foppery: foolishness, imbecility, stupidity, folly (*obsolete*).

form: in the scholastic philosophy, the essential determinant principle of a thing, that which makes anything (matter) a determinate species or kind of being.

fribble *sb.*: a trifling, frivolous fellow, easily beguiled, like Messer Nicia in Machiavelli's *Mandragola* (1520) or Mr Fribble in Shadwell's *Epsom-Wells* (1673).

frig: to masturbate.

gewgaw: splendidly trifling; showy without value (Johnson 1755).

give away: give up, resign, surrender (*rare*).

give over: desist, leave off.

glory: praise, honour, or admiration accorded by common consent to a person; a state of exaltation.

go for: pass as.

gossiping: a meeting of friends and acquaintances, especially at the birth of a child.

grace cup: the last cup of liquor drunk before retiring, a parting draught.

green-sickness: an anaemic disease, often characterized by morbid appetite for chalk, coal, etc., which affects young women about the age of puberty.

groat: a coin (1351–1662) worth four old pence.

gruntling: a low grunt.

handled: taken hold of (figuratively), examined, sized up.

hard-favoured: having an aspect harsh or unpleasant (*OED*); ugly (*AND*).

hard-pinched-for: stolen with difficulty (apparently Rochester's coinage); cf. *OED*, **Pinch**, *v.* 15a.

heart: a jewel or ornament in the shape of a heart.

heats: a redness or eruption on the skin, accompanied by a sensation of heat.

heretofore: in time past.

horseman's weight: the weight of a jockey in stones (14 lb = 1 stone).

huff: one puffed up with conceit of his own importance, valour, etc.; one who blusters or swaggers, a hector, a bully (*obsolete*).

idle: empty, vacant.

ignis fatuus: 'A phosphorescent light seen hovering or flitting over marshy ground . . . called Will-o'-the wisp. . . . When approached, the *ignis fatuus* appears to recede, and finally to vanish, sometimes reappearing in another direction. This led to the notion that it was the work of a mischievous sprite intentionally leading benighted travellers astray' (*OED*).

impertinent: irrelevant; not consonant with reason; absurd, idle, trivial, silly.

importance comfortable: a wife (*AND*).

incommode: inconvenient, troublesome.

infamy: public reproach, shame, or disgrace; the loss of all or certain of the rights of a citizen.

insolent: offensively familiar.

insult on: manifest arrogant or scornful delight over, upon, or on an object of scorn (*obsolete*).

intrench: encroach or trespass upon.

jade: a term of reprobation applied to a woman.

japan: of, belonging to, native to, or produced in Japan; fashionable, exotic, 'whatever is not common' (30.59).

jingling: playing with words for the sake of sound.

job: a portion of some substance.

Jowler: here the name of a dog, but a jowler is a breed of heavy-jawed dogs, like basset hounds and mastiffs.

kickshaw: (a corruption of the French *quelque chose*) a fancy, insubstantial French dish.

kindly: in an easy, natural way.

kindness: kind feeling; a feeling of tenderness or fondness; affection, love.

knack: a trick, a device, artifice; formerly often a deceitful or crafty device; a mean or underhand trick.

knight of the elbow: a gambler.

ladies of the town: prostitutes.

lawn sleeves: sleeves of fine linen, part of the episcopal dress.

leg: an obeisance made by drawing back one leg and bending the other.

libel: a verse satire.

limber: limp.

lime: impregnate a bitch; copulate with.

linkboy: a boy employed to carry a torch made of tow and pitch to light passengers along the streets.

livelong: an emotional intensive of *long*, used of periods of time.

loose: free from moral restraint; lax in principle, conduct, or speech; immoral; not tightly drawn, slack.

love-convicted: overcome with love.

lumpish: stupidly dull, heavy, or lethargic.

magazine: a place where goods are laid up; a storehouse (now *rare*).

make: making or manufacture.

make away: destroy, dispose of, get rid of.

matter: physical or corporeal substance, contradistinguished from immaterial or incorporeal substance (spirit, soul, mind).

memento mori: (Latin) remember that you have to die; a warning of death.

mere: pure, unmixed (*obsolete*).

mutton: a woman (*AND*).

nice: precise, strict, careful; strange, rare, uncommon (*obsolete*); reluctant, unwilling (*obsolete*); refined, cultured. 'In many examples from the 16th and 17th centuries it is difficult to say in what particular sense the writer intended the word to be taken' (*OED*).

noise: reputation (*obsolete*).

nokes: a ninny or fool.

onset: attacking an enemy.

owl: 'Applied to a person in allusion to . . . appearance of gravity and wisdom (often with implication of underlying stupidity)' (*OED*).

owned: acknowledged.

parts: abilities, capacities, talents; also *absolutely*, high intellectual ability, cleverness, talent; a euphemism for genitals.

pathetic: producing an effect upon the emotions. 'The sense of "miserably inadequate" is not recorded before 1937' (*OED*).

pea-straw: the stalks and leaves of the pea-plant.

pintle: penis.

pit: the floor of a theatre; the theatre audience. 'The Pit . . . is fill'd with Benches without Backboards, and adorn'd and cover'd with green Cloth. Men of Quality, particularly the younger Sort, some ladies of Reputation and Vertue, and abundance of Damsels that hunt for Prey, sit all together in this place, Higgledy-piggledy' (Henri Misson, *M. Misson's Memoirs and Observations in his Travels over England* (1719), 219).

play: gambling.

play booty: join with confederates in order to victimize another player; play or act falsely so as to gain a desired object; (*proverbial*) (Tilley B539).

plead: urge as a plea.

pledge: something given as a sign or token of favour or as an earnest of something to come.

posy: 'A syncopated form of *Poesy*, a short motto, originally a line or verse of poetry inscribed within a ring' (*OED* cites *Hamlet* (1603), II ii 162: 'Is this . . . the Poesie of a Ring?').

precise: strict or scrupulous in religious observance; in the 16th and 17th centuries, 'puritanical' (*OED*); foolishly scrupulous (*AND*).

presently: without any delay, at once, immediately.

pretending: professing falsely, feigning.

primitive: original, as opposed to derivative.

prodigious: unnatural, abnormal, monstrous.

proper: belonging to oneself, own (*archaic*).

prove: show to be such as is asserted or claimed; find out or learn, or know by experience; have experience of.

provision: something provided or arranged in advance.

Pug: here the name of a monkey, but 'pug' is a colloquial term for 'monkey'.

purely: without blemish, corruption, or uncleanness; faultlessly, guilelessly, innocently.

puzzling: (*transitive*) laboriously trying to puzzle something out; (*intransitive*) bewildering, confusing (*OED* cites Thomas Sherlock, *Several Discourses Preached at the Temple Church* (1734), 42: 'Mysteries . . . to puzzle the Minds of Men').

qualm: a fit of sickening fear, misgiving, or depression.

ramble: a walk in search of sexual partners; cf. 'Take you your Ramble, Madam, and I'll take mine' (Lee 1954, II 2).

recreation: comfort produced by something affecting the senses or body (*obsolete*).

refined: characterized by the possession of refinement in manners, action, or feeling; having a high degree of subtlety, nicety, or precision.

reforming: forming a second time.

rook: a cheat, swindler, or sharper, especially in gaming.

sad: sorrowful, mournful; grace, serious (*obsolete*).

salt-swol'n: in heat.

saucy: insolent towards superiors, presumptuous.

scarf: a broad band of silk worn by military officers across the body from one shoulder to the opposite hip.

scorbutic spots: ulcerations of the skin symptomatic of scurvy (vitamin C deficiency); 'by how much they encline to blackness, so much the worse' (Everard Maynwaring, *Morbus Polyrhizos* (1669), 51).

screw: to force or strain, as by means of a screw.

secure: to make free from care or apprehension; to free from doubt; to make one feel secure of or against some contingency (*obsolete*).

sense: intelligence, especially as bearing on action or behaviour.

serail: seraglio, apartments reserved for wives and concubines.

severe: rigorous in one's treatment of or attitude towards offenders.

shade: the visible but impalpable form of a dead person; the total darkness before God said, 'Let there be light' (Genesis 1.3).

shore: sewer.

shrug: move the body from side to side as a gesture of joy or self-satisfaction; fidget about.

sillery: an expensive wine produced in and around the village of Sillery in Champagne.

slur: the sliding of a die out of the box so that it does not turn (*obsolete*) (*OED*); a cheat at dice (*AND*).

sot: a foolish or stupid person (*obsolete*).

spend: to ejaculate; to have an orgasm.

sponge: various species of porifers used in bathing.

sprittle staff: properly a spittle-staff or mattock, 'A staff of wood four or five feet long, shod at the lower end with a wedge-like piece of iron, to *stub* thistles with' (James O. Halliwell, *A Dictionary of Archaic and Provincial Words*, 2 vols. (1847), II 785).

sprung: of game birds: made to fly up.

squab: a raw, inexperienced person (*obsolete*); short, fat person.

on the **square**: in a fair, honest, or straightforward manner; without artifice, deceit, fraud, or trickery.

stand: take up an offensive or defensive position; to await an onset; of the penis: to become erect.

stew: brothel.

still: continually, constantly, always.

stint: allotted amount, allowance.

stir: make any movement, move at all or in the least.

stone: a morbid concretion in the bladder, etc.

stout: valiant, brave, undaunted.

strangury: a disease of the urinary organs characterized by slow and painful urination (*OED*); 'pissing by drops' (Culpeper 1652, 49).

strike: cause a person to be overwhelmed or seized with terror, amazement, grief, or, rarely, love.

such: as much.

surfeit water: a medicinal drink for the cure of surfeit, a 17th-century Bromo-Seltzer.

swain: a man of low degree, a farm labourer, a countryman, a rustic (*archaic*).

swinger: a vigorous performer (*obsolete*); a person who is sexually promiscuous.

swive: copulate with.

take up: adopt.

take upon: put on airs.

take upon oneself: behave presumptuously or haughtily, assume airs (*obsolete*).

tawdry: dressed in cheap and pretentious finery (*OED*); 'gawdy, with lace or mismatched and staring colours' (*AND*).

tearing: violent, headstrong.

on **tick**: on credit.

tierce: a third of a pipe, or 14 gallons (of French claret in this case). 'Tierce claret' may be a phrase like 'draught beer'.

trade: the practice of some occupation, business, or profession habitually carried on, especially when practised as a means of livelihood or gain, frequently in a depreciatory sense.

trading: tradesmanlike, perhaps 'With sinister implication: [driving] a trade in something which should not be bought or sold' (*OED*).

treat: carry on negotiations with a view to settling terms.

trim: cheat a person out of money, in this case by selling a spavined horse.

true-love knot: a kind of knot of a complicated and ornamental form (usually either a double-looped bow or a knot formed of two loops intertwined), used as a symbol of true love.

truth: faithfulness, fidelity (now *rare* or *archaic*).

try: have the experience of: undergo, go through (*obsolete*).

twat: the female pudendum.

unblest: sexually unsatisfied; cf. 'the blest Lover' (Pope 1939–67, II 205).

undo: unfasten the clothing of; ruin by seducing.

use: utility, advantage, benefit.

vassal: subject, subordinate.

whiffling: trifling, insignificant.

whimsey: a fantastic or freakish idea; a capricious notion or fancy.

whitewash: a cosmetic wash used for imparting a light colour to the skin (*obsolete*).

withdrawing room: a private chamber attached to a more public room.

women coursers: dealers in women (*OED* cites Beaumont and Fletcher, *The Captain* (1613), V i: 'I am no Bawd, nor Cheater, nor a Courser / Of broken-winded women').

women fairs: places for the sale (*lit.* or *fig.*) of women.

worn: in fashion.

Notes

The Bible is quoted in the authorized King James version, the classics in the Loeb Classical Library (Harvard University Press and Heinemann), and Shakespeare in *The Norton Facsimile [of] The First Folio*, ed. Charlton Hinman (1968).

To His Sacred Majesty (Virtue's triumphant shrine, who dost engage)

2 *pilgrimage*: to Dover to greet the fleet bringing Charles II back to England: 'it being endlesse to reckon or number those that are gone, who are the flower of the Gentry of *England*, all striving to exceed each other in costliness of their Furniture and Equipage' (*The Publick Intelligencer*, 21–28 May 1660).

3 *ecstatic*: punning on two meanings of the word: the etymological sense of 'out of place', 'Out of themselves' (l. 4) and the lexical sense of 'intensely pleasurable' (*OED*) (Rochester 1984, 229).

5 *one camp*: the Lord General George Monck ordered the Parliamentary army, that defeated Charles II at Worcester in 1651, to march out of London on 23 May 1660 and to encamp at Blackheath, beyond Greenwich in Kent. 'At Black Heath the Army was drawn up where His Majesty viewed them, giving out many expressions of His Gracious favor to the Army, which were received by loud shoutings and rejoycings' (*The Parliamentary Intelligencer*, 28 May–4 June 1660).

7 *loyal Kent*: in 1648 a widespread insurrection in Kent on behalf of Charles I was savagely suppressed by Fairfax.

8 *Fencing her ways*: on Tuesday 29 May 1660 'His Majesty took his journey from Rochester betwixt four and five in the morning, the Military forces of Kent lining the wayes, and maidens strewing herbs and flowers, and the several towns hanging out white sheets' (*Mercurius Publicus*, 24–31 May 1660); *moving groves*: '2 or 300 Maids of the Town [Pursely, Kent] ... marched in Rank and File, each carrying a green Beechen bough, with Drums and Trumpets, up to Stinchcomb Hill, where ... they drank the Kings Health upon their Knees' (ibid.); cf. *Macbeth*, V v 38: 'MESSENGER: ... may you see it comming. / I say, a moving Grove'.

10 *sedentary feet*: punning on two meanings of the phrase: 'idle feet' and 'halting verse' (Rochester 1984, 229).

11 *youth*: Rochester was thirteen on 10 April 1660; *not patient*: impatient, 'Restlessly desirous, eagerly longing' (*OED*).

16 *father's ashes*: Henry Wilmot, 1st Earl of Rochester, died on 19 February 1658 at Ghent. He was buried first in Sluys, in the Netherlands, and was reinterred at Spelsbury, Oxfordshire.

To his Mistress (Why dost thou shade thy lovely face? Oh, why)

This is a parody of Francis Quarles, *Emblemes* (1635), 149–50, 170. By changing the order of the stanzas and a few words and phrases – 'My love' for 'My God' – Quarles's passionate poem of sacred love is turned into an equally passionate poem of profane love.

19–21 'Stanza xi of Quarles's *Emblemes*, III vii reads as follows: "If that be all, shine forth and draw thee nigher; / Let me behold, and die, for my desire / Is phoenix-like, to perish in that fire." In Rochester, this becomes: "If that be all Shine forth and draw thou nigher. / Let me be bold and Dye for my Desire. / A *Phenix* likes to perish in the Fire." There are only two verbal substitutions here of any consequence: . . . "behold" into "be bold", and the most striking introduction of the word "likes" in Rochester's versions of the third line. Otherwise, the transformation has been effected by means which are not properly linguistic: by end-stopping the second line where Quarles had permitted an enjambment and by a change in punctuation and accentual stress which suddenly throws the erotic connotations of the word "die" . . . into relief. . . . The lines are the same and not the same; another voice is speaking Quarles's words, from another point of view' (Righter 1968, 58).

23 *flameless*: the copy-text reads 'shameless', but the context requires Quarles's word.

27 *lamb . . . stray*: cf. 'it is not the will of your Father which is in heaven, that one of these little ones should perish' (Matthew 18.14).

35 *thy*: the copy-text reads 'my', but the context requires Quarles's word; cf. line 1.

36 *die*: cf. 'the LORD . . . said, Thou canst not see my face: for there shall no man see me, and live' (Exodus 33.20).

43 *thy*: the copy-text reads 'my', but the context requires Quarles's word.

Verses put into a Lady's Prayer-Book (Fling this useless book away)

This poem is an adaptation of two poems of Malherbe.

Writ in Calista's Prayer-Book. An Epigram of Monsieur de Malherbe

Whilst you are deaf to love, you may,
Fairest *Calista*, weep and pray,
And yet, alas! no mercy find;
Not but God's mercifull, 'tis true,
But can you think he'll grant to you
What you deny to all mankind?
(Charles Cotton, *Poems on Several Occasions* (1689), 51)

Written in Clarinda's Prayer-Book

In vain, *Clarinda*, Night and Day
For Mercy to the Gods you Pray:
What Arrogance on Heav'n to call
For that, which you deny to All!
(George Granville, Lord Lansdowne, *Poems upon Several Occasions* (1712), 124)

8 *Without repentance*: cf. 'O God . . . Restore thou them that are penitent' (*The Book of Common Prayer* (1683), sig. B1r).

16 *easy steps*: 'There is no source in Malherbe for Rochester's ideas of a sensual *gradus ad Parnassum*. . . . The metaphor was probably familiar to Rochester from Socrates' speech in the *Symposium* but in the anti-religious context of the poem it is made to provide an ironic commentary on its Christian application, exemplified in Crashaw's title *Steps to the Temple* and in Adam's words to Raphael in *Paradise Lost*, Book V, "In contemplation of created things / By steps we may ascend to God"' (Treglown 1973, 45–6).

17 *joys . . . above*: the phrase recurs in a poem of which the attribution to Rochester is confirmed (12.22).

Rhyme to Lisbon (Here's a health to Kate, our sovereign's mate)

'The . . . E. of Roch[ester] coming in . . . when the K. Charles was drinking Lisbon ["A white wine produced in the province of Estremadura in Portugal" (*OED*)], They had bin trying to make a Rhime to Lisbon, Now saies the K. here's one will do it. Rochester takes a glass, and saies A health to Kate! . . .' (B.L. MS. Add. 29921, f. 3v). For these extemporaneous verses Rochester employed a common ballad stanza, $A^4B^3A^4B^3$, with double rhyme in the short line. It can be sung to the tune of 'Chevy Chase' (Simpson 1966, 96).

1 *Kate*: Catherine of Bragança.

3 *Hyde*: Edward Hyde, Earl of Clarendon, was blamed for negotiating Charles's marriage to 'a barren Queen'; *bishop*: Gilbert Sheldon, Archbishop of Canterbury, married Charles and Catherine of Bragança at Portsmouth on 21 May 1662.

4 *of his bone*: cf. the solemnization of matrimony: 'we are members of [the Lord's] body, of his flesh, and of his bones. For this cause . . . they two shall be one flesh. This is a great mystery' (*The Book of Common Prayer* (1683), sig. K 12r).

Song (Give me leave to rail at you)

A reply to Rochester's verses, in Elizabeth Malet's hand with corrections in her hand, is preserved in Nottingham MS. Portland Pw V 31, f. 12r:

> *Song*
>
> Nothing adds to love's fond fire
> More than scorn and cold disdain.
> I to cherish your desire
> Kindness used, but 'twas in vain.
> 5   You insulted on your slave;
> To be mine you soon refused.
> Hope not then the power to have
> Which ingloriously you used.
>
> Think not, Thyrsis, I will e'er
> 10   By my love my empire lose.
> You grow constant through despair,
> Kindness you would soon abuse.

> Though you still possess my heart,
> Scorn and rigor I must feign.
15 > There remains no other art
> Your love, fond fugitive, to gain.
>
> You that cou'd my *Heart* subdue,
> To new *Conquests* ne're pretend,
> Let your example make me true,
20 > And of a Conquer'd *Foe*, a *Friend*:
> Then if e're I shou'd complain,
> Of your *Empire*, or my *Chain*,
> Summon all your pow'rful *Charmes*,
> And sell the *Rebel* in your *Armes*.

2 *scorn and ... disdain*: cf. 'LADY WISHFORT: ... a little Disdain is not amiss; a little Scorn is alluring' (Congreve, *The Way of the World* (1700), III 164–5).

9–10 *love ... empire*: the speaker refuses to cast herself as heroine in a Restoration heroic drama; cf. 'ZEMPOALLA: Were but this stranger kind, I'd ... give my Empire where I gave my heart' (Sir Robert Howard and John Dryden, *The Indian Queen. A Tragedy* (1664), IV i 55–6). Since Elizabeth Malet was an heiress, 'worth ... 2500*l.* per annum' (Pepys, 28 May 1665), her 'empire' was no fiction.

24 *sell*: Walker emends 'sell' to 'fell' (Rochester 1984, 22); 'quell' may be the word intended; cf. quell a rebellion.

From Mistress Price, Maid of Honour to Her Majesty, who sent [Lord Chesterfield] a Pair of Italian Gloves (My Lord, These are the gloves that I did mention)

Nicholas Fisher points out that the poem adopts the three-part structure and dramatic situation of Ovid's *Heroides* (375), but unexpectedly puts the woman in complete control of the situation (*Classical and Modern Literature* 11 (1991), 341–3).

7 *Bretby*: Bretby Park was the Chesterfield estate in Derbyshire.

Under King Charles II's Picture (I, John Roberts, writ this same)

1 *writ*: in the obsolete sense of 'draw the figure of (something)' (*OED*).

3 *by name*: Rochester may be mimicking Roberts's actual speech or mocking the traditional English carol: 'That there was born in Bethlehem, / The Son of God by name'; 'born of a virgin, / Blessed Mary by name' (*Oxford Book of Carols*, ed. Percy Dearmer *et al.* (1928), 25, 62).

To his more than Meritorious Wife (I am by fate slave to your will)

1–2 *I am by fate slave to your will | And shall be most obedient still*: the 'hyperbolic compliment' (303) of the first two lines is undercut by the comic double rhymes, 'compose ye ... a posy', 'duty ... true t'ye', and 'speeches ... breeches' (pronounced 'britches'), that follow.

8 *Yielding ... the breeches*: surrendering the authority of a husband (Tilley B645).

10 *Jan*: Rochester's surviving letters to his wife are signed 'Your humble servant Rochester' or 'R'.

Rochester Extempore (And after singing Psalm the 12th)

1 *Psalm the 12th*: Psalm 12, signed T[homas] S[ternhold] begins: 'Help, Lord, for good and godly men / do perish and decay: / And faith and truth from worldly men / is parted clean away' (Sternhold and Hopkins, *The Whole Book of Psalms, Collected into English Metre* (1703), sig. A4r).

6 *I am a rascal, that thou know'st*: Defoe quotes this line in the *Review* of 14 February 1713, attributing it to 'Lord Rochester's Confession to his Penitentials'; *rascal*: this ancestor of Robert Burns's Holy Willie is equally 'fash'd wi' fleshly lust'.

Spoken Extempore to a Country Clerk after having heard him Sing Psalms (Sternhold and Hopkins had great qualms)

1 *Sternhold and Hopkins*: Thomas Sternhold (d. 1549) and John Hopkins (d. 1570) collaborated to produce a metrical version of the Psalms (*c.* 1549) which survived in the next age as the standard for bad poetry (Thomas Brown, *The Works* (1711), IV 163–5).

The Platonic Lady (I could love thee till I die)

This exercise in octosyllabic couplets is an adaptation of some verses attributed to Petronius (Oldham 1987, 462):

> ### *A Fragment from Petronius Translated*
>
> Doing, a filthy pleasure is, and short;
> And done, we straight repent us of the sport:
> Let us not then rush blindly on unto it,
> Like lustfull beasts, that onely know to doe it:
> For lust will languish, and that heat decay.
> But thus, thus, keeping endlesse Holy-day,
> Let us together closely lie, and kisse,
> There is no labour, nor no shame in this;
> This hath pleas'd, doth please, and long will please; never
> Can this decay, but is beginning ever.
>   (Jonson 1925–52, VIII 294)

The title is ironical. What the lady advocates is not platonic love, 'free from sensual desire' (*OED*), but *coitus reservatus* (Sanskrit *karezza*), in which 'by a technique of deliberate control [i.e. 'the art of love' (l. 6)] . . . orgasm is avoided and copulation thereby prolonged' (*OED*, s.v. **coitus**).

7 *enjoyment*: ejaculation, which 'Converts the owner to a drone' (l. 12).

11–12 *sting . . . gone . . . drone*: cf. 'If once he lose his *sting*, he grows a *Drone*' (Cowley, *Against Fruition* (1668), 32).

17 *what*: penis.

23–4 *Let's practise then and we shall prove / These are the only sweets of love*: Possibly a parody of Marlowe's 'Come live with mee and be my love, / And we will all the pleasures prove' (*The Passionate Pilgrim* (1599), sig. D5) (Rochester 1953, 228).

Song (As Cloris full of harmless thought)

23 *the lucky minute*: cf. 'Twelve is my appointed lucky Minute, when all the Blessings that my Soul could wish Shall be resign'd to me' (Aphra Behn, *The Lucky Chance* (1686?; 1687), 58); 'Lovers that . . . in the lucky Minute want the Pow'r' (Samuel Garth, *The Dispensary* (1699), *POAS*, Yale, VI 735). Treglown isolates a lucky Minute/happy Time/Shepherd's Hour sub-genre of seventeenth-century erotic lyric and cites examples including Sir Carr Scrope's song in *The Man of Mode* (1676) (cf. headnote above), John Glanvill's *The Shepherd's Hour* (1686), and Dryden's song in *Amphitryon* (1690), IV i: *A Pastoral Dialogue betwixt Thyrsis and Iris* (Treglown 1982, 86-7). 'The Lucky Minute' also became a popular tune title (Simpson 1966, 106).

Song to Cloris (Fair Cloris in a pigsty lay)

8 *ivory pails*: the rarity and expensiveness of ivory (£167 per hundredweight in 1905) makes these ivory swill buckets a refinement of mock-epic proportions, like the ivory gate through which Cloris's false dream reaches her (*Odyssey*, XIX 562; *Aeneid*, VI 895).

15 *Flora's cave*: the cave in which the Greek nymph Chloris is raped by Zephyrus, the west wind, and from which she emerges as Flora, the Roman goddess of flowers and spring (Ovid, *Fasti*, V 195). The cave is Ovid's and the hymeneal gate may be Shakespeare's (*The Winter's Tale* (1609-10; 1623), I ii 196-8), but the phallic pig appears to be Rochester's.

31 *piercèd*: one reader wishes that this dream of rape had been a real rape 'perhaps' (Felicity Nussbaum, *The Brink of All We Hate* (1972), 62); *zone*: literally 'any encircling band' (*OED*, citing Francis Quarles, *Emblemes* (1635), 274: 'untie / The sacred Zone of thy Virginity'), cf. Aphrodite's zone which creates 'the lucky minute' (21.²23) for anyone wearing it (*Iliad*, XIV 214-16, trans. Richmond Lattimore, 'the elaborate, pattern-pieced / zone . . . [the] passion of sex is there'); figuratively that part of the body around which a girdle is fastened; cf. pelvic girdle.

39 *legs*: the moral disorder is reflected in a rhyming disorder, 'frigs . . . pigs . . . legs', that is unique in the poem.

40 *innocent and pleased*: *virgo intacta* and sexually satisfied.

To Corinna (What cruel pains Corinna takes)

7 *the silly art*: coyness, 'Affected rules of honour' (l. 12).

9 *tyrant*: virtue.

13 *she*: Corinna.

Song (Phillis, be gentler, I advise)

2 *Make . . . time*: 'The poem is identical in form, length and, it at first seems, subject matter, to the famous lyric recalled by the second line, Herrick's "To the Virgins, to make much of Time" . . . Yet there could not be a greater difference between them in substance or in tone . . .; while Herrick's poem is rooted in the present . . . Rochester's cruelly anticipates what is in store in the future: faded beauty, scandal, ruin, and death' (Treglown 1980, 24).

4 *time to repent*: Rochester's alleged deathbed repentance is described in Parsons 1680, 1–37.

15–16 *Die with the scandal of a whore, / And never know the joy*: quoted in Defoe, *An Elegy on the Author of the True-Born-English-Man* (1704), 32.

22–3 *joys . . . improved by art*: cf. 97.16n. and 'All that art can add to love' (46¹24).

Could I but make my wishes insolent

Although the poem has been called an epistle, it is not an epistle. Lines 1–6 address the reader about 'her' (l. 6) in the third person. Lines 7–26 address her in the first person, 'you . . . your' (ll. 11, 17, 26). Lines 1–6 are a kind of proem to the dramatic monologue that follows. After ll. 14–16 the switching of skirts can be heard.

6 *lay hold of her*: cf. 'lay hold on her, and lie with her' (Deuteronomy 22.28).

7–8 *spirit . . . merit*: imperfect rhyme and the unique double rhyme make this couplet outstanding in the poem. The metre, stretching out 'fa-MIL-i-AR' over two full iambs, makes this the outstanding word in the couplet. 'Familiar' is what the speaker designs to be.

9 *blundering . . . Phaëton*: the son of Helios (the sun) and Klymene, 'foolish Phaëton . . . doest desire . . . A greater charge than any God coulde ever have' (Ovid, *Metamorphoses* (1567), f. 15), namely, to drive the chariot of the sun. The horses bolted and Phaëton was destroyed.

15 *what he next must say*: cf. 'think what next to say' (26.113).

The gods by right of nature must possess

In the opening speech of Shadwell's *The Virtuoso* (25 May 1676; 1676) Bruce, the hero, apostrophizes 'great *Lucretius*', the patron saint of gentlemen of wit and sense like Bruce himself and Shadwell and Shadwell's friend Rochester. 'Almost alone', Bruce says, Lucretius demonstrates 'that Poetry and Good Sence may go together' (Shadwell 1927, III 105).

5–6 *Rich in themselves, to whom we cannot add, / Not pleased by good deeds nor provoked by bad*: cf. 'ipsa suis pollens opibus, nil indiga nostri, / nec bene promeritis capitur neque tangitur ira' ('[divinity] . . . strong by its own strength, needing nothing from us, neither propitiated by worship nor aroused by anger') (Lucretius, *De rerum natura*, II 650–51); cf. '[Rochester] could not see that there was to be either reward or punishment' (Burnet 1680, 52); cf. 23.3–5.

To Love (O Love! how cold and slow to take my part)

The translation of Ovid's *Amores*, II ix provides a kind of bill of fare for Rochester's major love poems, which celebrate not the acts but the mishaps of love, 'Love's fantastic storms' (l. 37): premature ejaculation (15), falling in love with a whore (21.125), the fear of inadequacy (43.¹9–10), falling in love with an old man (45).

Epigraph: the first line of Ovid's *Amores*, II ix: 'O Cupid, who never can be sufficiently reviled'.

4 *They murder me*: cf. 'They flee from me, that sometime did me seeke' (Sir Thomas Wyatt in *Songs and Sonnets* (1585), f. 22r.

9 *give o'er*: leave behind the birds taken and press on for more.

13–14 *disarmed . . . disarmed*: Rochester imitates the Ovidian 'turn', as Dryden called it, but not the striking Ovidian image: 'in nudis . . . / ossibus? ossa mihi nuda' (on naked bones . . . my bones naked) (*Amores*, II ix 13–14).

15 *dull*: without love; the word translates Ovid's phrase 'sine amore'; *scornful maids*: cf. 'she who scorns a Man, must die a Maid' (Pope 1939–67, II 197).

17–18 'Since *Roma* and *Amor* are palindromes, Ovid may be making the witty point that their opposite behaviour is natural' (Francis Cairns, in *Creative Imitation and Latin Literature*, ed. David West *et al.* (1979), 126).

21–2 *whore . . . to be a bawd*: '[Ovid's] images of ships laid up in dock and of a retired gladiator exchanging his sword for a practice foil are replaced by the distinctively Restoration' whore who graduates to a bawd (Love 1981, 143).

25 *in Celia's trenches*: Rochester's phrase has no counterpart in Ovid, but does occur in *Priapea*, XLVI 9: 'fossas inguinis ut teram dolemque' (labour in that ditch between your thighs); cf. 'said my uncle *Toby* – but I declare, corporal, I had rather march up to the very edge of a trench – A woman is quite a different thing – said the corporal. – I suppose so, quoth my uncle Toby' (Sterne 1940, 583).

44–50 cf. *in lazy slumbers blest /. . . happy. . . whilst I believe*:

> And slumbring, thinks himselfe much blessed by it.
> Foole, what is sleepe but image of cold death,
> Long shalt thou rest when Fates expire thy breath.
> But let me crafty damsells words deceive,
> Great joyes by hope I inly shall conceive.
>   (C[hristopher] M[arlowe], *All Ovids Elegies* [*c.* 1640], sig. C5r)

60 *vassal world*: Rochester (but not Ovid) closes the poem by bringing it back to Rome's 'wide world' (l. 17): if Cupid could make women love, his domination of the world of lovers would be as complete as Rome's domination of the world of nations.

The Imperfect Enjoyment (Naked she lay, clasped in my longing arms)

A poem on the premature ejaculation mishap was almost an obligatory exercise for the Restoration poet. George Etherege, Aphra Behn, William Congreve, and three anonymous poets cranked out examples, but Rochester's is the funniest.

1 *Naked she lay*: 'She lay all naked in her bed' was the title of a popular tune (Simpson 1966, 657).

3–4 *equally inspired . . . eager fire, / . . . kindness . . . flaming . . . desire*: heightened interest and intensity in Rochester's verse are frequently accompanied by heightened sound effects, particularly assonance ('equally . . . eager', 'inspired . . . fire . . . kindness . . . desire') and alliteration ('fire . . . flaming'); cf. 'balmy brinks of bliss' (l. 12) and 'I . . . alive . . . strive: / I sigh . . . swive' (ll. 25–7).

18 *Her hand, her foot, her very look's a cunt*: cf. *The Conquest of Granada I* (December 1670; 1672), III i 71: 'Her tears, her smiles, her every look's a Net' (Dryden 1956– , XI 47) (Treglown 1976, 555).

19 *Smiling*: decorum does not permit her to laugh.

22–3 '*Is there then no more?*' / *She cries*: cf. 'Why mock'st thou me she cry'd?' (C[hristopher] M[arlowe], *All Ovids Elegies* [*c.* 1640], sig. E2v).

23 *this*: foreplay.

23–4 *love . . . pleasure*: 'We'd had more pleasure had our love been less' (Etherege, 1963, 8).

27 *I sigh, alas! . . . but cannot swive*: in the Garden of Eden 'Each member did their wills obey' (43.7); cf. 'How just is Fate . . . / To make him *Love* the *Whore* he cannot *Please*' (Defoe, *The Dyet of Poland* (1705), *POAS*, Yale, VII 119).

29 *shame*: cf. 'To this adde shame . . . / The second cause why vigour faild me' (Marlowe, op. cit., sig. E2r).

30 *impotent*: both rhyme scheme and metre require that the third syllable be fully accented, 'IM-po-TENT', prolonging and emphasizing the crucial word in the poem.

31 *her fair hand*: cf. 'Her touch could have made Nestor young again' (Ovid, *Amores*, III vii 41).

45 *withered flower*: cf. 'member . . . more withered than yesterday's rose' (Ovid, *Amores*, III vii 65–6). Rochester omits Ovid's nice detail of the prostitute thoughtfully spilling water so her maid would not know of her client's failure, and substitutes the frightful curse, which is not in Ovid. When he is rescued from Orgoglio's dungeon, the Red Crosse knight is 'Decay'd, and al his flesh shronk up like withered flowres' (Spenser, *The Faerie Queene* (1590), I viii 41) (John H. O'Neill, *Tennessee Studies in Literature* 25 (1980), 63).

46 *base deserter of my flame*: cf. 'nefande destitutor inguinum' (unspeakable deserter of my loins) (Tibullus 1971, 174). The transition from history of the recreant member to apostrophe to the recreant member (ll. 46–72) may recall Marvell's *An Horatian Ode upon Cromwell's Return from Ireland* (1650; 1681) which also moves from history of a recreant Member (ll. 1–112) to apostrophe to a recreant Member (ll. 113–20).

48 *magic*: cf. 'Why would not magic arts be the cause of my malfunction?' (Ovid, *Amores*, III vii 35).

50 *oyster, cinder, beggar*: apparently shorthand for oyster-wench, cinder-woman, London beggar; cf. 'Oyster, Beggar, Cinder Whore' (Defoe, *Reformation of Manners* (1702) (*POAS*, Yale, VI 408).

54–7 *hector in the streets* / . . . *hides his head*: Quaintance suggests that these lines expand Remy Belleau's phrase, 'Brave sur le rempart et couard à la brèche' (Bold on the battlements, coward in the breach) (*PQ* 42 (1963), 191).

54 *hector*: in June 1675 Rochester 'in a frolick after a rant [a bombastic speech] did . . . beat downe the dyill which stood in the middle of the Privie [Gard]ing, which was esteemed the rarest in Europ' (Davies 1969, 351). Whereupon John Oldham wrote *A Satyr against Vertue* 'Suppos'd to be spoken by a Court-Hector at Breaking of the Dial in Privy Garden' (Oldham 1987, 57–67; cf. Marvell 1927, I 310). Rochester's words on the occasion have been preserved: 'Rochester, lord Buckhurst, Fleetwood Shephard, etc. comeing in from their revells. "What!" said the earl of Rochester, "doest thou stand here to [fuck] time?" Dash they fell to worke' (Aubrey 1898, II 34).

56–7 *if his king . . . claim his aid, / The . . . villain shrinks*: Rochester did not volunteer for service in the third Dutch War (1672–4); cf. 3.17–18.

62 *Worst part of me*: cf. 'pars pessima nostri' (worst part of me) (Ovid, *Amores*, III vii 69).

On King Charles (In the isle of Great Britain long since famous grown)

Although the custom of fosterage was no longer institutional at the Stuart court, Charles II gave Rochester an allowance of £500 a year while he was at Oxford, chose Dr Andrew Balfour to be his travelling governor, received Rochester at Whitehall upon his return from his travels, provided him lodgings in the palace, appointed him gentleman of the bedchamber with a pension of £1,000 a year for life, and chose for his wife a most sought-after heiress who also wrote verse. In all this the King manifestly acted as foster-father (Ronald Paulson, in *The Author in His Work*, ed. Louis L. Martz and Aubrey Williams (1978), 117). In his juvenile verse Rochester acknowledged that he owed much more than 'cold respect' (3.15) to this distant figure.

The relation between the two, therefore, is the old love–hate business of father and son. Whereas the precocious boy wanted nothing more than to throw away his life for his king the disillusioned adult regarded Charles with 'a mixture of irony, contempt and genuine affection' (Pinto 1962, 75).

4 *easiest*: cf. 'This Principle of making the *love* of *Ease* exercise an entire Sovereignty in his Thoughts, would have been less censured in a private Man, than might be in a Prince' (Halifax, 1912, 204) (Rochester 1982, 86).

5 *no ambition*: cf. 'the profuseness, and inadvertency of the King hath saved *England* from falling into destruction' (*A Letter to Monsieur Van B— de M— at Amsterdam, written Anno 1676 by Denzil Lord Holles concerning the Government of England* [1676?], 5–6).

6 *the French fool*: Charles II was negotiating a separate peace with the Dutch (see next note), but Louis XIV carried on the war for four more years.

8 *Peace*: 'our King ... being always most willing to hear of peace' (Roger Palmer, Earl of Castlemaine, *A Short and True Account of the Material Passages in the late War between the English and Dutch*, 2nd ed. (1672), 47), negotiations with the Dutch were opened during the winter of 1672–3 and the Treaty of Westminster was signed on 19 February 1674. The sexual pun on peace/piece could not have displeased Charles II.

11 *length*: Pepys heard about the King 'hav[ing] a large - - - - -' (Pepys, 15 May 1663); cf. 'his *Majesty* [is] the most potent Prince in Christendom' (Carew Reynel, *The True English Interest* (1674), sig. A6r). The length of Charles's sceptre was two feet, ten and a half inches (Rochester 1982, 86).

13 *brother*: James, Duke of York.

14 *I hate all monarchs*: neither this nor its antithesis, 'I loathe the rabble' (68.120) provides evidence of Rochester's political orientation.

14–15 *I hate all monarchs ... Britain*: Vieth (Rochester 1968, 61), Walker, and some of the ms. copies put these lines at the end of the poem, 'although this gives the poem a perhaps too defiantly republican slant' (Rochester 1984, 75, 271). But six ms. copies and the copy-text put the lines here, allowing the poem to close with the diminished sexuality of Charles II's 'declining years' (ll. 25–33). The reaction to '*all* monarchs' comes more appropriately here at the end of the contrast between Charles II and Louis XIV.

25 *declining years*: Charles was forty-three on 29 May 1673.

29 *hang an arse*: 'hold back' (*OED*).

32 *hands ... thighs*: cf. 'my advice to [Nell Gwyn] has ever been this ... with hand, body, head, heart and all the faculties you have, contribute to his pleasure all you can' (Rochester to Henry Savile, June 1678, Rochester *Letters* 1980, 189).

A Ramble in St James's Park (Much wine had passed with grave discourse)

The meaning of 'ramble' dilucidated below (*Title*) is essential to understanding the dramatic situation assumed in the opening lines of the poem. There is no reason to identify the speaker with Rochester, who would be unlikely to prowl in St James's Park 'unaccompanied by . . . a purse bearer, a page, and a couple of footmen' (Love 1972, 161). The *chagrin d'amour* of this aristocratic speaker (101. Headnote) is that he has fallen in love with a whore with whom he is presently cohabiting (ll. 107–32). An historical analogue to this dilemma is provided by the cohabitation of Edward Mountagu, Earl of Sandwich, with Betty Becke, 'a common Courtizan', so damaging to Sandwich's reputation that Samuel Pepys felt compelled to write 'a great letter of reproof' to his patron and kinsman (Pepys, 22 July 1663, 18 November 1663).

Now drunk and overwhelmed with lust for his whore, Rochester's imagined speaker sallies forth in search of her, i.e. 'rambles' in St James's Park (where presumably he knows that she patrols). He catches up with her just as Corinna picks up three clients and drives off with them in a hackney coach (l. 82), to the speaker's unspeakable frustration.

Title *Ramble*: to go looking for a sexual partner; cf. 'RANGER. Intending a Ramble to St. James's Park to night, upon some probable hopes of some fresh Game' (Wycherley 1979, 24) (John D. Patterson, *N&Q* 226 (1981), 209–10).

4 *the Bear*: the Bear and Harrow in Bear Yard off Drury Lane (Rochester 1984, 263) was said to be 'an excellent ordinary after the French manner' (Pepys, 18 February 1668).

7 *St James's Park*: a deer park enclosed with a brick wall, created by Henry VIII and improved by Charles II. The Mall was a wooded alley for playing a mallet game, the Canal was made by damming a tributary of the Thames, and the famous trysting place was the heavily wooded area around Rosamund's Pond in the south-west corner of the Park.

9 *James*: presumably James the son of Zebedee, the first apostle to be martyred, whose remains are venerated at Santiago de Compostela.

10 *consecrate*: cf. 'how lovingly the Trees are joyned . . . as if Nature had design'd this Walk for the private Shelter of forbidden Love' (Colley Cibber, *Love's Last Shift* (1696), III ii 2).

19 *mandrakes*: Rochester's fancy that mandrake grows up from semen spilled on the ground is a variant of the folklore motif (*Motif-Index* A2611.5) that mandrake grows up from blood spilled on the ground.

20 *fucked the very skies*: cf. 'aged trees / . . . invade the sky' (*On St. James's Park, as lately improved by his Majesty* (1661) (Waller 1893, 170).

22 *Aretine*: About 1524 in Rome Marcantonio Raimondi published sixteen engravings after drawings by Giulio Romano of sixteen positions or 'postures' of sexual intercourse (afterwards called *I Modi*). Pope Clement VII insured that this became an extremely rare book by ordering Raimondi to be imprisoned and the plates and copies of Raimondi's book to be destroyed. After effecting Raimondi's release, Pietro Aretino (1492–1556), 'the scourge of princes', wrote sixteen *Sonetti Lussoriosi* to illustrate a second edition of Raimondi's prints (*c.* 1525) and then fled to Florence. Although Rochester may have been able to buy a copy of this book when he visited Italy (1662–4), no copy of either edition is now known. But about 1527 and probably in Venice a pirated edition of *I Modi* with Aretino's sonnets was published and of this edition one copy survives in private hands. A facsimile of this book with English translations of

Aretino's sonnets was edited by Lynne Lawner and published by Northwestern University Press in 1988. Posture 15 is reproduced below.

23-4 *shade ... made*: cf. 'Methinks I see the love that shall be made, / The Lovers walking in that Amorous shade' (*On St. James's Park, as lately improved by his Majesty* (1661) (Waller 1893, 168) (Rochester 1984, 263)).

26 *Whores*: of the lowest and highest class. A bulker was a streetwalker who performed on the bulkheads in front of shops. An alcove was a recess in a bedroom for a bed of state (*OED*).

33 *walks*: there were walks along Pall Mall, on both sides of the Canal, and around Rosamund's Pond.

37 *charming eyes*: cf. 'eyes, / ... make ... men their prize' (*On St. James's Park as lately improved by his Majesty* (1661) (Waller 1893, 169)).

44 *tails*: 'The simile comparing Corinna to a bitch in heat recurs throughout the poem' (Paulson 1972, 28).

49-50 *Sir Edward Sutton*: These lines may be alluded to in Dorset's *Colin* (1679): 'Chance threw on him Sir Edward Sutton, / A jolly knight that rhymes to mutton' (*POAS*, Yale, II 168); *Banstead*: Banstead Downs in Surrey, about fifteen miles south of London, was 'covered with a short grass intermixed with thyme, and other fragrant herbs, that render the mutton of this tract ... remarkable for its sweetness' (*London and Its Environs Described*, 6 vols. (1761), I 246); *mutton*: 'loose women' (*OED*). 'He loves laced mutton' is proverbial (Tilley M1338). This is a quibble that Shakespeare found equally irresistible: 'The Duke (I say to thee againe) would eate Mutton on Fridaies' (*Measure for Measure* (c. 1604; 1623), III ii 192).

67-8 *comedy ... landlady*: the first of a series of comic rhymes: 'arse on ... parson' (ll. 91-2), 'fraternity ... of buggery' (ll. 145-6). The grammatical construction here is elliptical: 'from' is omitted before 'the comedy'.

77-8 *kiss ... 'Yes'*: the dissonant rhyme reflects the 'anatomical distortion' in the couplet (Farley-Hills 1978, 111).

97 *natural freedoms*: cf. '[Rochester] thought that all pleasure, when it did not [hurt another or injure one's health], was to be indulged as the gratification of our natural Appetites. It seemed unreasonable to imagine these were put into a man only to be restrained, or curbed' (Burnet 1680, 38).

101 *a whore in understanding*: Mistress Flareit likewise comes to regard her affair with a fool, Sir Novelty Fashion, as a 'forfeiture of my Sense and Understanding' (Colley Cibber, *Love's Last Shift* (1696), IV i 52).

102 *fools*: the word receives heavy rhetorical emphasis as the first term of a crucial contrast with porters and footmen (l. 120). The speaker's incredulity is emphasized by an incomplete sentence.

114 *Drenched*: 'like Juvenal's Messalina' (Vieth and Griffin 1988, 60).

116 *digestive surfeit water*: the speaker's rage may be expressed by redundancy: the phrase is redundant (surfeit water is a digestive) and ll. 117-22 are redundant (they replicate ll. 113-16).

119 *devouring cunt*: cf. *Motif-Index* F547.1.1 Vagina dentata.

133-66 The pronouncement of the curse on Corinna (*Motif-Index* M410) is a specialized form of ordaining the future, a kind of malign prophecy. Satire in turn may be a specialized form of pronouncing curses, not on Corinna, of course, but on the system of which Corinna is a sympton.

136 *in ... fools delight*: cf. 'a Woman who is not a Fool, can have but one Reason for associating with a Man that is' (Congreve 1967, 399).

138 *go mad for the north wind*: to fall in love with Boreas, whose sexual exploits include turning himself into a horse, would correspond with the speaker's mishap in falling in love with Corinna.

142 *perish*: in orgasm.

143–50 These are the impossible tasks of folklore (*Motif-Index* H1010) which add up to an emphatic 'never'.

160 *dog-drawn bitch*: When a dog and bitch are locked together in mating, the dog may throw a hind leg over the bitch's back and try to pull away, dragging the bitch behind him with great pain to both (Paulson 1972, 28–9).

165–6 *And may no woman better thrive | Who dares profane the cunt I swive*: cf. 'May no man share the blessings I enjoy without my curses' (Rochester *Letters* 1980, 123, to Elizabeth Barry).

Song (Love a woman? You're an ass)

3 *happiness*: an outrageous chore is emphasized by an outrageous comic rhyme with 'You're an ass' (l. 1).

4 *idlest*: Harvard MS. Eng. 636F, p. 247 and Rochester 1691, 44, derived from it, reads 'silliest', but 'idlest', the reading of the copy-text, meaning 'empty, vacant' (*OED*), enforces the geographic image of 'God's creation'.

9 *Farewell, woman!*: cf. 'Two Paradises 'twere in one / To live in Paradise alone' (Marvell 1927, I 49). Both Marvell and Rochester are bluffing.

Seneca's Troas, *Act 2. Chorus* (After death nothing is, and nothing, death)

1 *After death nothing is, and nothing, death*: Rochester translates the first line literally: 'Post mortem nihil est ipsaque mors nihil' (Seneca, *Troades*, 397); cf. 'Nil igitur mors est ad nos ... scilicet haud nobis quicquam' (Therefore death is nothing to us ... nothing at all will be able to happen to us) (Lucretius, *De rerum natura*, III 830, 840).

8 *become ... lumber*: cf. 'maior enim turbae disiectus materiai / consequitur ... materies opus est ut crescant postera saecla' (a greater dispersion of the disturbed matter takes place at death ... matter is needed that coming generations may grow) (ibid. III 928–9, 967).

10 *Where ... things unborn are kept*: 'quo non nata iacent' (where they lie who were never born) (Seneca, *Troades*, 408).

11 *Devouring time swallows us whole*: 'A few phrases from ... *Troades englished*, by Samuel Pordage, published in 1660 while Rochester was still at Wadham, seem to have remained in his mind: "*Time* us, and *Chaos*, doth devour" [l. 11], "*Body* and *Soul*" [l. 12], and "idle tailes" [l. 17]' (Rochester 1984, 255).

13–18 *Hell and the foul fiend ... | Are senseless stories ... | Dreams*: 'Taenara et aspero / regnum sub domino limen et obsidens / custos non facili Cerberus ostio / rumores vacui verbaque inania / et par sollicito fabula somnio' (the underworld, the savage god who rules the dead, and the dog Cerberus who guards the exit, are empty words, old wives' tales, the stuff of bad dreams) (Seneca, *Troades*, 402–6); cf. 'nil esse in morte timendum ... nec quisquam in barathrum nec Tartara deditur atra ... nec miser inpendens magnum timet acre saxum / Tantalus, ut famast ... nec Tityon volucres ineunt Acherunte iacentem' (there is nothing to be feared after death ... There is no wretched Tantalus, as the story goes, fearing the great rock that hangs over his head ... No Tityos lying in Acheron is ravaged by winged creatures)

(Lucretius, *De rerum natura*, III 866, 966, 980–81, 984); *no more*: cf. 'there is no naturall knowledge of mans estate after death; much lesse of the reward that is then to be given . . . but onely a beliefe grounded upon other mens saying' (Hobbes 1935, 100). Rochester told Burnet that 'he could not see there was to be either reward or punishment' after death (Burnet 1680, 52).

Tunbridge Wells (At five this morn when Phoebus raised his head)

Tunbridge Wells, about thirty miles south-east of London, is the site of chalybeate springs supposed to have medicinal properties. It became a fashionable resort after visits by King Charles and Queen Catherine (Pepys, 22 July 1663) and by the Duke and Duchess of York with the Princesses Mary and Anne in 1670.

The poem seems experimental in several ways at once. It may be a parody of the Virgilian loco-descriptive poem, examples of which include *To Penshurst* (1616), with its 'walkes for health as well as sport' (Jonson 1925–52, VIII 93) and Waller's reprise, *At Penshurst* (1645) (Waller 1893, 46). But its speaker seems pointedly un-Georgic. He is 'querulous, foul-mouthed, and dyspeptic, and in no sense . . . to be identified with [Rochester]' (Love 1972, 153). He is in fact a perfect satyr, more sympathetic with the equine than with the human race (ll. 183–5).

1 *At five*: cf. 'the morning, when the Sun is an hour more or lesse high, is the fittest time to drink the water' (Rowzee 1671, 53).

3 *trotted*: cf. 'the nearest good lodgings were at Rusthall and Southborough, a mile or two distant from the wells' (Rochester 1968, 73).

14 *a stag at rut*: 'the allusion is almost certainly to Sir Robert Howard, who had made himself ridiculous with his pompous poem, *The Duel of the Stags*' (1668) (Robert Jordan, *ELN* 10 (June 1973), 269). Rochester's friend Henry Savile wrote a parody of Sir Robert's poem entitled 'The Duel of the Crabs' (i.e. of the crab lice) (*The Annual Miscellany for the Year 1694: Being the Fourth Part of Miscellany Poems* (1694), 293–7).

16 *Sir Nicholas Cully*: Sir Nicholas, a booby squire, is tricked into marriage with the cast mistress of a London fop in Etherege's first comedy, *The Comical Revenge: or Love in a Tub* (1664). The role was created by James Nokes.

24 *crab-fish*: crabmeat, an aphrodisiac? cf. Tilley C785.

31 *Endeavouring*: the metre stretches out 'en-DEAV-our-ING' into four syllables as the speaker strains to avoid the two knighted fools.

38–9 *A tall, stiff fool . . . | The buckram puppet*: cf. 'He takes as much care and pains to *new-mold* his *Body* at the *Dancing-Schools*, as if the onely *shame* he fear'd were the retaining of that *Form* which *God* and *Nature* gave him. Sometimes he walks as if he went in a *Frame*, again as if both head and every member of him *turned* upon *Hinges*. Every step he takes presents you with a perfect Puppit-play' (Clement Ellis, *The Gentile Sinner, or, England's Brave Gentleman: Characterized* (1660), 30) (David Trotter in Treglown 1982, 125).

40 *as woodcock wise*: proverbial (Tilley W746).

44 *intrigues*: one seventeenth-century spelling, 'intregues', may indicate how the word was pronounced: 'IN-tregues'.

52 *Scurvy, stone, strangury*: Tunbridge water was supposed to be specific for genito-urinary diseases and scurvy (Rowzee 1671, 41, 42).

54 *wise*: the context requires 'wise' to mean 'fashionable'. This nonce meaning is not recorded in *OED*, but pushing words beyond the range of their current meanings is Rochester's practice.

58 *ambassadors*: cf. 'the mystery of the gospel, For which I am an ambassador' (Ephesians 6.19–20) (Rochester 1982, 89).

59 *pretend commissions given*: apostolic succession, 'the continued transmission of the ministerial commission, through an unbroken line of bishops from the Apostles onwards' (*OED*).

65 *Bayes*: Samuel Parker; *his importance comfortable*: Rochester mocks Parker's coy reference to his wedding plans as 'Matters of a closer and more comfortable importance to my self' (Parker, *Bishop Bramhall's Vindication* (1672), sig. A2r) (Rochester 1968, 75–6). Marvell wonders 'What this thing should be' and concludes that 'it must be . . . a Female' (*The Rehearsal Transpros'd* (1672), 7–8). The mockery is reinforced by the comic rhyme, 'all this rabble . . . comfortable'.

66 *archdeaconry*: Parker was appointed archdeacon of Canterbury in June 1670.

67 *trampling on religious liberty*: In *A Discourse of Ecclesiastical Polity* (1670) (and two later works), Parker assumes an extreme Erastian position, warning 'how Dangerous a thing Liberty of Conscience is' (xlvi) and arguing that the unstable nature of man made it 'absolutely necessary . . . that there be set up a more severe Government over mens Consciences and Religious perswasions, than over their Vices and Immoralities' (xliii). He concludes that 'there is not the least possibility of setling a Nation, but by Uniformity in Religious Worship' (325).

70 *Marvell*: this is Rochester's only surviving reference to the man who said that 'the earle of Rochester was the only man in England that had the true vaine of satyre' (Aubrey 1898, II 54).

72 *distemper*: Parker complains that he was 'prevented by a dull and lazy distemper' from replying sooner to *The Rehearsal Transpros'd* (*A Reproof to the Rehearsal Transpros'd* (1673), 1). Marvell assumes that the distemper was venereal (*The Rehearsal Transpros'd: The Second Part* (1673), 8–9) (Rochester 1968, 76). Tunbridge water was specific for 'running of the reines, whether it be *Gonorrhea simplex* or *Venerea* . . . nay and the Pox also' (Rowzee 1671, 46–7).

74 *sweetness*: according to the humours theory (not yet discredited in the seventeenth century), choler was bitter, melancholy sour, blood sweet, etc.; cf. Burton, *The Anatomy of Melancholy* (1621), Part I, Section 1, Member 2, Subsection 2.

76 *Importance*: presumably Parker's fiancée or wife; see l. 65n. above.

79 *sisters frail*: 'whores' (l. 5).

82 *gypsies*: 'even the late L. of *Rochester* . . . was not ashamed to keep the *Gypsies* Company' (*AND*, sig. A8v).

90 *conventicle*: pronounced 'CON-ven-TIC-le' (*OED*). Dryden rhymes 'roar and stickle . . . Conventicle' (Prologue to *The Disappointment* (1684), 71).

98 *The would-be wit*: Sir Robert Howard(?) (l. 18).

99 *scrape of shoe*: 'to avoid the horrible absurdity of setting both Feet flat on the Ground, when one should always stand tottering on the Toe, as waiting in readiness for a *Congée*' (*News from Covent Garden; or, The Town-Gallants Vindication* (1675), 6).

101 *ruffled foretop*: the hair on the crown of a wig dressed in frills.

110 *It is your goodness, and not my deserts*: cf. 'MISS: My Lord, that was more their Goodness, than my Desert' (Swift 1939–68, IV 155).

116 *cribbage fifty-nine*: having moved her scoring pegs through fifty-nine of the sixty holes on the cribbage board, she was unable to advance to the sixtieth and final 'game hole' (Rochester 1968, 77).

123 *a Scotch fiddle*: 'The itch' (*OED*) of sexual excitement; cf. 'a Tailor might scratch her where ere she did itch' (Shakespeare, *The Tempest* (1611; 1623), II ii 55).

135–6 *a barren | Woman . . . fruitful*: cf. 'there is nothing better against barrenness, and to make fruitful, if other good and fitting means, such as the several causes shall require, be joyned with the water' (Rowzee 1671, 48).

142 *those*: menstrual periods.

149 *fribbles*: cf. 'MRS BISKET: Ay, Mr. *Fribble* maintains his Wife like a Lady . . . and lets her take her pleasure at *Epsom* two months together. | DOROTHY FRIBBLE: Ay, that's because the Air's good to make one be with Child; and he longs mightily for a Child: and truly, Neighbour, I use all the means I can' (*Epsom Wells* (1673), II i; Shadwell 1927, II 128) (Robert L. Root, Jr., *N&Q* 221 (May–June 1976), 242–3).

152 *enlarge*: by the addition of cuckold's horns.

153 *Cuff and Kick*: 'Two cheating, sharking, cowardly Bullies' in *Epsom Wells*, which opened at Dorset Garden on 2 December 1672. In the fifth act, Doll Fribble and Molly Bisket are discovered in bed with Cuff and Kick, respectively.

157 *reputation*: Gaston Jean Baptiste, comte de Cominges, the French ambassador (1663–65), was not so gullible. The queen is still at Tunbridge, he reported to Louis XIV in July 1663, 'ou les eaux n'ont rien produit ce qu'il l'en avait espère. On peut les nommer les eaux de scandale, puisqu'elles, on pense, ruinent les femmes et les filles de reputation' (where the waters have done nothing of what was expected of them. Well may they be called the waters of scandal, for they nearly ruined the good names of the maids of honour and of the married women who were there without their husbands) (J. J. Jusserand, *A French Ambassador at the Court of Charles the Second* (1892), 89).

158 *generation*: 'CUFF: Others come hither to procure Conception. | KICK: Ay, Pox, that's not from the Waters, but something else that shall be nameless' (Shadwell 1927, II 107).

165 *With hawk on fist*: this was Rochester's father's disguise, or cover, in his dramatic rescue of Charles II after the defeat at Worcester in 1651 (Clarendon 1707, III 326).

167–9 Rochester's scorn for the cadets' posturing is reflected in the scornful rhymes, 'horse . . . purse . . . arse'.

172 *Bear Garden ape*: the Hope theatre on the Bankside in Southwark reopened in 1664, featuring the blood sports that the Puritans abominated: bull- and bear-baiting, dog- and cock-fights. Pepys found it 'good sport . . . But . . . very rude and nasty' (Pepys, 14 August 1666). Evelyn agreed that it was a 'rude & dirty passetime'. Evelyn also mentions 'the Ape on horse-back' that ended the evening's performance (Evelyn, 16 June 1670).

176 *what thing is man*: cf. 'Lord, what is man that thou of him | tak'st such abundant care?' (Sternhold and Hopkins, *The Whole Book of Psalms* (1703), sig. A3r) (Treglown 1973, 46–7).

180–81 *Thrice happy beasts . . . | Of reason void*: cf. 'Thrice happy then are beasts . . . | They only sleep, and eat, and drink, | They never meditate, nor think' (Thomas Flatman, *Poems and Songs* (1674), 139) (Thormählen 1988, 404n.); *foppery*: except for the outlawed gypsies and the Bear Garden ape, everyone in the poem falls under the speaker's dictum of 'foppery', in the extended sense of self-promoting pretence. Although he is called 'the young gentleman' (l. 175), the Bear Garden ape does not pretend to be a man.

182 *remorse*: in the context the word retains something of its etymological meaning, 'biting back' (David Trotter in Treglown 1982, 126), encapsulating the satyr-speaker's response to what he sees and hears at Tunbridge Wells.

Artemisa to Chloe. A Letter from a Lady in the Town to a Lady in the Country concerning the Loves of the Town (Chloe, In verse by your command I write)

7 *adventurers for the bays*: cf. 'How vainly men themselves amaze / To win the Palm, the Oke, or Bayes' (Marvell 1927, I 48).

7–8 *adventurers... returns*: overseas traders ... profits.

17 *Bedlam has many mansions*: cf. 'In my father's house are many mansions' (John 14.2).

20 *discreetly*: the net meaning clear of irony is 'self-destructively'.

24 *arrant*: an intensifier 'without opprobrious force' (Rochester 1984, 278).

40 *the most generous passion*: Artemisa's experience in this field (l. 38) suggests that this line be read ironically, articulating Artemisa's suspicion that love may be a totally selfish, self-absorbing, *un*generous passion.

40–42 *Love ... | The safe director*: a major irony of the poem. Artemisa has lost love (l. 38), Corinna is 'Cozened ... by love' (l. 191) and degraded, the booby squire is 'faithful in his love' (l. 230) and destroyed.

44 *That cordial drop*: cf. 'The Cordial Drop of Life is Love alone' (Pope 1939–67, IV 245).

46–7 *raise... subsidies*: increase the amount ... of grants.

52–3 *it ... that*: love ... play, i.e. love now employs as many cheats as gambling.

55 *'Tis*: the antecedent is the 'trade' (l. 51) of love.

57 *gypsies*: 'A contemptuous term for a woman, as being cunning, deceitful, fickle' (*OED*) (Rochester 1984, 278). But Artemisa is making another point as well: she observes that women of her class, enjoying all the freedom possible in an ordered society, will nevertheless turn outlaw for the freedom to achieve infamy, which entails the loss of the freedoms enjoyed in an ordered society. Artemisa frames this argument pointedly in an ordered triplet. The choice of infamy is a perverse exercise of free will.

58 *hate ... infamy*: Dustin Griffin suggests 'hate restraints, even the restraint of avoiding infamy'.

59 *They*: women who do not live for love (l. 50) by 'nature's rules' (l. 60), but who trade in love.

64 *'Tis below wit ... to admire*: the Horatian commonplace, 'nil admirari' (*Epistles*, I vi 1); cf. 'not to be brought by anything into an impassioned state of mind, or into a state of desire or longing' (Charlton T. Lewis and Charles Short, *A Latin Dictionary* (1962), 40).

72 *that with their ears they see*: i.e. not at all.

83 *had been*: i.e. 'would have been' (Rochester 1980, 92).

96 *let me die*: the identifying speech tag of Melantha, a heroine in Dryden's *Marriage à la Mode* (April 1672?; 1673). 'A Court-Lady' in this play is named Artemis. In the dedication of the play to him Dryden acknowledges that it 'receiv'd amendment' from Rochester, who also 'commended it to the view' of the King (Dryden 1956– , XI 221). Rochester's 'amendments' may have concerned the character of Melantha, whom the fine lady resembles in her affectation (Rochester 1968, 106n.).

98 *Embarrassée*: cf. 'Melantha: ... *embarrass* me! what a delicious *French* word' (Dryden 1956– , XI 300).

99 *Indian queen*: *The Indian Queen*, the first rhymed heroic play, by Sir Robert Howard and John Dryden, opened at the Theatre Royal in January 1664. It seems unlikely that the fine lady 'had turned o'er' (l. 162) this play, for neither of the queens, Amexia and Zempoalla, are 'Rude and untaught'.

103–4 *à la mode, | ... incommode*: cf. 'Un poète à la cour fut jadis à la mode; / Mais des fous aujourd'hui c'est la plus incommode' (Poets used to be in fashion at court, but today they are the most troublesome fools) (Boileau, *Satire* I, 109-10) (Davies 1969, 354).

108-9 *With searching wisdom, fatal to their ease,* | *They'll still find out why what may, should not please*: cf. 'His wisdom did his happiness destroy, | Aiming to know that world he should enjoy' (47.33-4) (Rochester 1984, 279); *They'll still find out why what may, should not please*: although 'ten low Words' do creep in this one line, the uncertainty in the third and fourth feet – are 'why' and 'may' stressed or unstressed? – the cacophony created by 'why what' and the internal pause between 'may, should' make the line anything but 'dull' (Pope 1937-67, I 278).

115 *The perfect joy of being well deceived*: cf. Ovid, *Amores*, II x (27.47-8); 'O yet happiest if ye . . . know to know no more' (Milton 1931-8, II i 134); '*Happiness . . . is a perpetual Possession of being well deceived*' (Swift 1939-68, I 108).

155-7 *the very top* / . . . *of folly we attain* / *By curious search*: cf. 'The most ingenious way of becoming foolish is by a system' (Anthony Ashley Cooper, 3rd Earl of Shaftesbury, *Characteristics* (1711), ed. John M. Robertson, 2 vols. (1900), I 189).

166-7 *good qualities . . . blest* / . . . *so distinguished*: 'the tone of irony' in these phrases has been noted (David Sheehan, *Tennessee Studies in Literature* 25 (1980), 77).

183-4 *an Irish lord . . . City cokes*: types of booby squire whom Corinna entraps.

194 *knew*: cf. 'Adam knew Eve his wife; and she conceived' (Genesis 4.1).

209 *Easter term*: one of the four times during the year (from seventeen days after Easter to the day after Ascension Day) when the law courts are in session.

213 *country*: 'a district . . . often applied to a county' (*OED*). 'My young master's . . . great family' rules the county by generous provision of 'strong ale and beef' at quarter sessions and general elections.

236-7 *complains,* | *Rails . . . maintains*: 'Corinna is the subject' (Rochester 1984, 281).

247 *poison him*: 'a conscious or unconscious daydream of disposing of her [the fine lady's] husband permanently rather than for an afternoon' (Sitter 1976, 296).

248 *in her . . . arms*: when *Artemisa to Chloe* is scored as an opera, this will be the climactic scene. On stage left of a divided stage in a dumb show the booby squire's lady and his children are turned away from the door by a servant in night dress. The squire's lady sinks to the stoop in exhaustion. As it begins to snow she rouses herself to gather the children to her and cover them with her cloak. In a simultaneous action on stage right in a second-floor bedroom the booby squire is discovered in bed with Corinna. He is beginning to feel the effects of poison that Corinna has put into his wine at dinner but rouses himself to sing a passionate aria proclaiming eternal love for Corinna and dies in her arms. She gets up and covers the body with the bed sheet.

261 *such stories I will tell*: cf. 'I dare almost promise to entertain you with a thousand bagatelles every week' (Dryden to Rochester, summer 1673, Rochester *Letters* 1980, 91).

261-4 *tell* | . . . *swell,* | . . . *hell;* | . . . *Farewell*: after 'a virtuoso display of poetic technique' (Howard Weinbrot, *Studies in the Literary Imagination* 5 (1972), 35) including half lines, half rhymes, single and double rhymes, end-stopped couplets, run-on couplets, and twelve triplets, Rochester ends with a unique, resounding quatrain.

Timon. A Satyr (What, Timon, does old age begin t'approach)

1 *A*: Auteur in Boileau, *Satire* III. If the parallel with Boileau were enforced, ll. 1–4 would be spoken by Rochester.

6 *th'Mall*: a walk bordered by trees in St James's Park; cf. 'Ibam forte Via Sacra, sicut meus est mos / nescio quid meditans nugarum, totus in illis. / accurrit quidam notus mihi nomine tantum, / arreptaque manu' (Horace, *Satire*, I ix 1–4) (I was strolling at random along the Via Sacra musing the way I do on some trifle or other and wholly intent thereon, when up runs a man I knew only by name and seizes my hand) (Rochester 1982, 92).

13–32 these lines have no counterpart in Boileau.

15 *the praise of pious queens*: may be the title of a moralizing broadside.

16 *Shadwell's unassisted . . . scenes*: even before *Epsom Wells* was performed, it was charged that 'the best part' (Shadwell 1927, II 278) had been written by Sir Charles Sedley. Despite Shadwell's repeated denials, the charge found its way into *Mac Flecknoe* (1676; 1682) (Dryden 1956–   , II 58).

35–6 *Huff, | Kickum*: almost a spoonerism for 'Cuff and Kick' (48.153).

39 *They will . . . fight*: introducing suspense into the narrative.

40 *tam Marte quam Mercurio*: on the verso of the title-page of *The Steel Glas. A Satyre* (1576) (Wood 1813–20, I 435–6), George Gascoigne included a portrait of himself in armour with this motto. Walter Raleigh wrote commendatory verses for this volume and after Gascoigne's death the motto was 'assumed by, or appropriated to' Raleigh himself (*Biographia Britannica* 1747–66, V 3467).

41 *I saw my error . . . too late*: cf. 'trop tard, reconnaissant ma faute' (seeing my mistake too late) (Boileau, *Satire* III, 37).

42–67 these lines have no counterpart in Boileau.

57 *the French king's success*: France and England declared war on the United Provinces in April 1672. In May the French army under the personal command of Louis XIV crossed the Rhine at Tolhuys and occupied three of the seven provinces. Louis XIV established his headquarters at Utrecht on 20/30 June (*London Gazette*, 20 June 1672) and was only prevented from marching into Amsterdam when William of Orange ordered the polders to be flooded (*A Narrative of the Progress of His Most Christian Majesties Armies against the Dutch* (1672)). The campaign of 1673 began with the successful reduction of Maastricht, which had been bypassed in 1672. 'The *French* Army go on Conquering and get all', Buckingham complained to the House of Lords in January 1674, 'and we get nothing' (Buckingham, *Miscellaneous Works* (1704), '3).

59 *two women*: Louise-Françoise de la Vallière (1644–1710) was a maid of honour to Henrietta Anne, Duchess of Orléans, when she became mistress of Louis XIV in 1661. Françoise-Athenais de Rochechouart (1641–1707) married the marquis de Montespan in 1663 and in July 1667 became a mistress of Louis XIV.

73 *champagne*: the copy-text spelling, 'Champoon', may indicate how the word was pronounced.

73–4 *French kickshaws . . . | Ragouts and fricassees*: cf. 'CLODPATE: I . . . spend not scurvy French kick-shaws, but much Ale, and Beef, and Mutton, the Manufactures of the Country . . . I hate *French* Fricasies and Ragousts' (*Epsom Wells* (December 1672; 1673), Shadwell 1927, II 112, 151).

78 *The coachman . . . ridden*: this ironic reversal is number 15 of Aretino's postures (*I Modi* 1988, 86).

80 *tool*: dildo; *countess*: Elizabeth, Countess of Percy.

84 *good cheer*: cf. a citizen's idea of a banquet, 'two puddings' (Pope 1939–67, III ii 119).

88 *Instead of ice*: cf. 'Point de glace, bon Dieu! dans le fort de l'été!' (No ice? Good God! In the middle of summer?) (Boileau, *Satire* III, 83).

91–2 *table . . . so large*: Boileau's diners were crowded (Boileau, *Satire* III, 53–4); *six old Italians*: where the host and hostess and five guests sat, there was room at the table for more than six Romans to *recline* (Rochester 1982, 93).

95–110 these lines have no counterpart in Boileau.

105 *virtuous league*: marriage or a discreet affair(?).

108 *taste their former parts*: one critic finds it impossible to determine whether the effect of the *double entendre* is 'malicious ridicule or amused sympathy' (Love 1972, 163), but the affect of the thirty-odd lines describing the hostess, as powerful as that of *A Song of a Young Lady. To her Ancient Lover*, seems incompatible with 'malicious ridicule'.

111 *ourselves*: Timon includes himself as object of satire, or 'acknowledg[es] the incompleteness of his isolation' (Treglown 1982, 83).

112 *regulate . . . the state*: cf. 'Chacun a . . . réformé l'Etat' (everyone . . . remakes the state) (Boileau, *Satire* III, 162–4). The zeugma, 'regulate the stage, and . . . state', is Rochester's invention.

114 *Mustapha and Zanger die*: they commit suicide in Act V of Orrery's *The Tragedy of Mustapha*, 'perhaps composed in half an hour' (68.97) and produced at Lincoln's Inn Fields on 3 April 1665.

117–18 Halfwit misquotes ll. 269–70 of Orrery's *The Black Prince*, which opened at the Bridges Street theatre on 19 October 1667: 'And which is worse, if worse than this can be, / She for it ne'er excus'd her self to me'. It was said to be 'the worst play of my Lord Or[r]ery's' (Pepys, 23 October 1667).

119 *There's fine poetry*: cf. 'C'est là ce qu'on appelle un ouvrage achevé' (That's what you call a finished work) (Boileau, *Satire* III, 195).

120 *So little on the sense the rhymes impose*: applied to Orrery the line may mean, Even in rhyme Orrery's verse remains prosy/prosaic. Applied to Rochester it may mean, Even in rhyme Rochester's verse retains colloquial word order and cadence; cf. '[Rochester] is the first poet in English to write satires . . . which, however artful their . . . rhymes, sound like someone talking' (Treglown 1982, 84).

125 *two . . . plays without one plot*: Etherege's *The Comical Revenge; or, Love in a Tub* (March 1664) and *She wou'd if she Cou'd* (February 1668) are the plays. The 'design' of the latter was found to be 'mighty insipid' (Pepys, 6 February 1668), but both plays have conventional comic plots.

126 *Settle, and Morocco*: Elkanah Settle's *The Empress of Morocco*, rivalling Dryden's heroic dramas, had two performances at court before the public opening at Dorset Garden on 3 July 1673. Rochester wrote a prologue for the second performance at court.

128–30 Huff misquotes *The Empress of Morocco*, II i 10, 61–2: 'Their lofty Bulks the foaming Billows bear . . . / *Saphee* and *Salli, Mugadore, Oran*, / The fam'd *Arzille, Alcazer, Tituan*'. Settle had a way with place-names like John Milton: 'Close sailing from *Bengala*, or the Isles / Of *Ternate* and *Tidore*' (*Paradise Lost* (1667, 1674), II 638–9).

132 *for Crowne declared*: Rochester began to patronize John Crowne in 1671. Crowne dedicated to Rochester his second play, *The History of Charles the Eighth of France* (November 1671; 1672) with engaging modesty: 'I have not the Honour of much acquaintance with your Lordship . . . I have seen in some little sketches of your Pen excellent Masteries . . . and . . . I have been entertained . . . with the wit, which your Lordship sprinkles . . . in your ordinary converse' (sig. a1v).

Posture 15, an engraving by Marcantonio Raimondi after a drawing by Giulio
Romano, reprinted in *I Modi*, ed. Lynne Lawner (1988), opposite p. 88.
(Photograph courtesy of Northwestern University Press.)

133 *the very wits of France*: including Gaultier de Coste, seigneur de la Calprenède,
Cassandra, the Fam'd Romance, trans. Sir Charles Cotterell (1652); Madeleine de
Scudéry, *Artamenes; or, The Grand Cyrus, An Excellent New Romance*, trans. F. G.
(1653–5); *Clelia. An Excellent New Romance*, trans. John Davies and C. Haven (1655–
6).

134 *Pandion*: Crowne's first publication was a prose romance modelled on Sidney's
The Countesse of Pembrokes Arcadia (1590) and entitled *Pandion and Amphigeneia, or,
The History of the Coy Lady of Thessalia* (1665).

138–40 Kickum quotes (correctly) *The History of Charles the Eighth of France* (1672),
II i 85–7.

144 *The Indian Emperour*: Dryden's fourth play, a sequel to *The Indian Queen*
(January 1664; 1665) with Sir Robert Howard, opened at the Bridges Street theatre in
April 1665.

145–6 the lines quoted (correctly) by Kickum are spoken by stout Cortez in *The Indian Emperour*, I i 3–4; Walter Scott also found them 'ludicrous' (Dryden 1882–93, II 319).

150 *laureate*: Charles II appointed Dryden poet laureate and historiographer royal on 18 August 1670.

152 *Souches*: for some weeks after 9 April 1674 it was expected in London that Ludwig Ratuit von Souches (1608–82), commander of the Imperial Army on the Rhine, would engage Turenne at the head of the French army. This expectation was dashed when the Imperial Army was diverted into Flanders (*London Gazette*, 8 June 1674) (Harold F. Brooks, *N&Q* 174 (May 1938), 384–5).

159–60 *courage . . . | 'Tis a short pride*: cf. '[No] Virtue . . . can we name, | But what will grow on Pride' (Pope 1939–67, III i 78).

168–9 *at t'other's head let fly | A greasy plate*: cf. 'Lui jette pour défi son assiette au visage' (He hurls his plate in his face as a challenge) (Boileau, *Satire* III, 214).

174 *Their rage once over, they begin to treat*: cf. 'Et, leur première ardeur passant en un moment, | On a parlé de paix et d'accommodement' (Their anger was soon dispersed and they began to talk of peace and accommodation) (Boileau, *Satire* III, 227–8).

A Dialogue between Strephon and Daphne (Prithee now, fond fool, give o'er)

31 *change*: cf. 'to be | *Constant*, in *Nature* were *Inconstancy*' (Cowley, *The Mistress* (1656), 19–20) (Rochester 1984, 231).

33–40 Since it has not always been understood (R. N. Parkinson, *Archiv für das Studium der Neueren Sprache und Literaturen* 207 (August 1970), 142), the tenor of this meteorological metaphor may be noted; it is love-making, from inflammatory foreplay to 'quiet' afterglow.

38 *Like meeting thunder we embrace*: because it is the only iambic tetrameter line in the last sixty-four lines of the poem and because of its imperfect rhyme, this line calls appropriate attention to itself as the climax of the sound effects of the poem and of the love-making within the metaphor.

50 *sincere*: the imperfect rhyme may call into question the sincerity of Daphne's successor; cf. ll. 55–6.

51 *Gentle, innocent, and free*: 'What Strephon means . . . is "promiscuous"' (Treglown 1980, 22).

68 *false*: critics wonder whether Daphne is lying (Righter 1968, 63; Treglown 1980, 22), raising the further possibility that the poem is a version of the Cretan Liar paradox.

71–2 *discovers . . . lovers*: the unique double rhyme points the moral of the fable, which is promptly annulled by the rest of the poem in which Strephon's deceit is so carefully balanced against Daphne's deceit that there is nothing to choose between them.

The Fall (How blest was the created state)

Basic to the mishaps of love is the anxiety of lovers, the fear of malfunction, against which Adam and Eve were secured in 'the created state'. The irony is one of which Milton would not have disapproved: by an act of disobedience to God, Adam and Eve forfeited the obedience of their own bodies. For purposes of the poem Rochester may have assumed something that he did not believe. 'He could not apprehend', he told Burnet, 'how there should be any corruption in the Nature of Man, or a Lapse derived from *Adam*' (Burnet 1680, 72). This fact may switch the tone of the poem from tragi-comic to straight comic.

1–2 *the created state / Of man and woman*: Rochester alludes to unfallen sexuality, cele-brated in Book IV of *Paradise Lost* (1667, 1674), 'Whatever Hypocrites austerely talk' (IV 744). But Milton says nothing about 'desire' or 'pleasure' until *after* the Fall (IX 1013, 1022) and of course never anything about 'members'.

8 *wish*: Marvell's wish was 'To live in Paradise alone' (Marvell 1927, I 49).

13–14 *duty* ... *| The nobler tribute*: cf. 'Returning thee the tribute of my dutie' (Samuel Daniel, *Delia* (1592), sig. B1r) (Thormählen 1988, 406n.); *a*: the copy-text reads 'my', but the indefinite article needed to complete the parallel, 'a heart ... a frailer part', survives in three manuscripts.

The Mistress (An age in her embraces passed)

1–2 *An age in her embraces* ... *| Would seem a winter's day*: Rochester may recall these lines in *The Mistress* about the opposite effect of love: '*Hours* of late as long as *Days* endure, | And very *Minutes*, *Hours* are grown' (Cowley 1905, 93), but the concept of value time, as expounded by E. M. Forster, is not unfamiliar: 'there seems something else in life besides time, something which may conveniently be called "value", something which is measured not by minutes or hours, but by intensity' (*Aspects of the Novel* (1927), 28). Sterne's novels are constructed on this principle: 'a colloquy of five minutes, in such a situation, is worth one of as many ages, with your faces turned towards the street' (Sterne 1928, 24); *a winter's day*: cf. 'lovers ... get a winter-seeming summers night' (Donne 1912, I 39).

5 *But oh, how slowly minutes roll*: the pause after 'oh' and the assonance, 'oh ... slow ... roll', make the sound imitate the sense.

7 *love* ... *is my soul*: cf. '*Love* which is ... *Soul* of Me' (Cowley 1905, 140).

12 *living tomb*: cf. 'in this [flesh] our living Tombe' (Donne 1912, I 258).

15 *shades of souls*: an impossibility; being immaterial, souls cast no shadows.

15–16 *On shades of souls and heaven knows what: / Short ages live in graves*: Time seems short in his mistress's embrace but very long in the intervals between embraces. Compared with the interminable length of time between embraces, the time spent in the grave (eternity) seems short: 'Short ages live in graves'.

26 *Love raised to an extreme*: cf. 'the extremities of ... Love' (Cowley 1905, 66).

32 *pain can ne'er deceive*: cf. Dostoyevsky's Underground Man who argues that if a man invariably chooses pleasure, he is an automaton, programmed for pleasure, 'a kind of piano key'. Only by choosing pain can a man 'confirm to himself ... that men are still men, and not piano keys' (*Notes from Underground*, trans. Mirra Ginsburg (1974), 26, 34).

A Song (Absent from thee I languish still)

7–8 *try | That tears*: i.e. 'undergo for tearing'; *That*: the antecedent is 'mind' (l. 6).

9 *When wearied with a world of woe*: 'certainly the worst line in Rochester' (Farley-Hills 1978, 80); cf. Tennyson, *Despair* (*The Nineteenth Century* 10 (November 1881), 631): 'were worlds of woe'.

15 *Faithless*: the most important word in the stanza is emphasized (1) by the substitution of a trochee for an iamb, (2) by alliteration, 'fall ... Faithless ... false ... unforgiven' (ll. 14–15), and (3) by internal rhyme, '*Lest* ... un*blest* ... Faith*less* to ... *rest*' (ll. 13–16).

NOTES TO PAGES 45–46

16 *my everlasting rest*: cf. 'here / Will I set up my everlasting rest' (*Romeo and Juliet*, V iii 109–10).

A Song of a Young Lady. To her Ancient Lover (Ancient person, for whom I)

Rochester imagines a young woman who has already committed herself to a man who is older but not yet 'Ancient': 'Long be it ere thou grow old', the girl says (Wilcoxon 1979, 147). By speaking in the person of the young woman, Rochester is able to avoid the judgemental tone of the paradox and to go beyond paradox to the amoral realm of low comedy 'that neither apportions blame nor gives approval' (David Farley-Hills, *The Benevolence of Laughter* (1974), 138; Edith Kern, *The Absolute Comic* (1980), 75).

The arrangement of the heptasyllabic couplets in stanzas of increasing length reduces the 'Song' element of the title but provides the vehicle for a submerged metaphor in the poem, as Vieth hints (*Tennessee Studies in Literature* 25 (1980), 48).

18 *From ... ice ... released*: the girl's 'art' restores 'nature' as May restores January every year; art and nature coalesce.

A Satyr against Mankind (Were I (who to my cost already am))

There is some point in retaining the old spelling 'Satyr' in the title of this poem. If it is a satyr speaking, then a creature half-man and half-animal is saying that he would rather be all animal. The urgent reasons that he gives for his choice constitute the argument of the poem. The conclusion of the argument, that the difference between the ideal man and the average man is greater than that between man and animal, or that most men are inferior to animals, is more pointed if spoken by a satyr. 'The bolder the better', as Swift said of paradoxes. 'But the Wit lies in maintaining them' (Swift 1939–68, II 101).

Another reason to retain the old spelling is to remind ourselves that the speaker of the poem is no more the Earl of Rochester (Davies 1969, 350–51) than he is Nicolas Boileau-Despréaux, whose *Satire* VIII (1668) is very distantly imitated in these verses. He is a personated figure, 'querulous, foul-mouthed, and dyspeptic', like the satyr-speaker in *Tunbridge Wells* (Love 1972, 153).

3 *spirit*: cf. 'For Spirits when they please / Can either Sex assume, or both ... in what shape they choose' (Milton 1931–8, II 23); *share*: a possible pun similar to part/privy part; the *os pubis* was called the share bone, and the share was the groin (*OED*, s.v. **Share**, *sb.*²).

5 *bear*: cf. '*Bears* are better / Then *Synod-men*' (Butler 1967, 97).

6 *anything but that vain animal*: cf. 'Make me anything but a man' (Menander, *Frag.* 23) (John F. Moore, *PMLA* 58 (June 1943), 399).

7 *so proud of being rational*: cf. 'An ill dream, or a cloudy day, has power to change this wretched creature, who is so proud of a reasonable soul' (Dryden, Dedication of *Aureng-Zebe* (17 November 1675; 1676) (Dryden 1882–93, V 199).

9 *sixth*: the sixth sense in this context is not 'a supposed intuitive faculty' (*OED*), but reason itself. Hobbes is certain that reason is *not* a sense: 'Reason is not as Sense ... borne with us ... but attayned by Industry' (Hobbes 1935, 25).

10 *certain instinct*: cf. 'Reason raise o'er Instinct as you can, / In this 'tis God directs, in that 'tis Man' (Pope 1939–67, II i 101).

12–14 *Reason, an ignis fatuus ... wandering ways it takes*: cf. 'Metaphors, and senselesse and ambiguous words, are like *ignes fatui*; and reasoning upon them, is wandering amongst innumerable absurdities' (Hobbes 1935, 26).

15 *fenny . . . thorny*: is Rochester parodying Milton's 'craggy . . . shaggy . . . mossy . . . mazy' pastoral vocabulary (Milton 1931–8, II i 48, 126; 114, 201, 158, II ii 281; II i 115, II ii 266)?

18–19 *from thought to thought*: cf. 'Mais l'Homme sans arrest, dans sa course insensée / Voltige incessament de pensée en pensée' (Boileau, *Satire* VIII, 35–6) (But sillier Man, in his mistaken way . . . / His restless mind rolls from thought to thought) Oldham 1987, 163); cf. 'Sinking from thought to thought' (Pope 1939–67, V 278); *falls headlong down / Into . . . boundless sea*: cf. 'c'est la voye par où il s'est precipitée à la damnation eternelle' (the way whereby man hath headlong cast himselfe downe into eternall damnation) Montaigne, *The Essays*, trans. John Florio (1603), 288; cf. 'Hurld headlong . . . down / To bottomless perdition' (Milton 1931–8, II i 10).

25–8 *Old Age and Experience . . . make him understand, / That all his life he has been in the wrong*: Goethe quotes 'jenem schrecklichen Texte' (those frightful words) in *Aus meinem Leben: Dichtung und Wahrheit* (1811–33), III xiii; Defoe quotes l. 28 only in the *Review*, 12 December 1704.

29 *Huddled in dirt*: cf. 'lodged here in the dirt and filth of the World' (Montaigne 1700, II 190); *engine*: a commonplace of contemporary medical theory, cf. We are 'forced therefore to consider the body of Man, not only as an Engine of curious and admirable workmanship . . . But also as a Machine' (Thomas Coxe, *A Discourse, wherein the Interest of the Patient in Reference to Physick and Physicians is soberly Debated* (1669), 276).

33 *wisdom did his happiness destroy*: cf. 'Knowing too much long since lost Paradise' (Suckling 1971, I 37) (Thormählen 1988, 402); 'happiest if ye seek / No happier state, and know to know no more' (Milton 1931–8, II i 134).

34 *that world he should enjoy*: cf. 'enjoy / . . . this happie state' (ibid., II i 162).

39 *threatening doubt*: fear (l. 45) that the joke is on them.

43 *escape*: i.e. when the joke is not on them (this time). Sir Carr Scrope may allude to these lines in *In Defense of Satire* (1677): 'Each knave or fool that's conscious of a crime, / Though he 'scapes now, looks for't another time' (*POAS*, Yale, I 368).

49 *Against . . . wit*: cf. 'these men . . . who turn all things into Burlesque and ridicule . . . are too witty . . . to embrace the principles of Christianity' (Thomas Smith, *A Sermon of the Credibility of the Mysteries of the Christian Religion* (1675, 10).

50–71 The adversary's argument is blunted by a series of imperfect rhymes: 'care . . . severe, heaven . . . given, soaring pierce . . . universe, there . . . fear'.

56 *grand indiscretion*: the speaker's attack on reason (ll. 8–30).

61 *everlasting soul*: Rochester 'thought it more likely that the Soul began anew' in the procreation of each person (Burnet 1680, 65).

62–3 *maker . . . from himself . . . did the image take*: cf. 'Soul that spiritual Image wherein the Divine likeness doth shine' (Nathaniel Ingelo, *Bentivolio and Urania* (1660), 238).

64–5 *in shining reason dressed / To dignify . . . above beast*: cf. 'not prone / And Brute as other Creatures, but endu'd / With Sanctitie of Reason' (Milton 1931–8, II i 229).

66–7 *Reason . . . beyond material sense*: cf. 'elevated beyond things of corporeal sense, [the mind] is brought to a converse and familiarity with heavenly notions' (Simon Patrick, *The Parable of the Pilgrim* (1664), 153) (Griffin 1973, 193).

67–9 *take a flight beyond material sense, / . . . pierce / The flaming limits of the universe*: cf. 'N'est-ce pas l'Homme enfin, dont l'art audacieux / Dans le tour d'un compass a mesuré les Cieux, / Dont la vaste science embrassant toutes choses, / A foüillé la nature, en a percé les causes' (Isn't it Man, whose reckless art, boxing the compass, has surveyed the heavens, whose learning without limits has explored Nature and penetrated into her first causes) (Boileau, *Satire* VIII, 165–8) (Rochester 1982, 108); *flaming limits of the universe*: cf. 'flammantia moenia mundi' (the flaming outworks of the world) (Lucretius, *De rerum natura*, I 73) (Rochester 1926, 356). The irony of having the clerical adversary quote 'the pagan and atheistic Lucretius' has not been lost (Griffin 1973, 192).

71 *true grounds of hope*: cf. 'That Immortality which lay hid in the dark guesses of Humanity, is here [in the Bible] brought to light, and all doubts concerning the Portion of Good men are resolved' (Nathaniel Ingelo, *Bentivolio and Urania* (1660), 214).

72–97 The speaker turns the tables on the adversary by arguing that it is not wit but 'glorious man' (l. 60) and 'shining reason' (l. 64) that is at fault (David Trotter, in Treglown 1982, 130).

73 *Ingelo*: Nathaniel Ingelo's *Bentivolio and Urania* (1660) is a prose romance in four books. There is no pricking on the plain, however, for Bentivolio (Good Will) and Urania (Heavenly Light) are brother and sister. Included in the work is both an utopia, Theoprepia (The Divine State), and a dystopia, Polistherion (City of the Beasts). In the former, the topics of casual conversation include 'The *Prudence* and *Fidelity* of *Vigilant Magistrates*, the *chearful Submissions* of *Loyall Subjects*, the *wise Deportment* of *Loving Husbands*, the *modest Observance* of *Obedient Wives*, the *indulgent Affections* of *Carefull Parents*, the *ingenuous Gratitude* of *Dutifull Children*, the *discreet Commands* of *Gentle Masters*, and the *ready Performances* of *Willing Servants*' (234).

74 *Patrick's Pilgrim*: Simon Patrick's *The Parable of the Pilgrim* (1665) begins with a vision of the heavenly city and concludes with the heavenly city itself, 'all built of . . . pretious stones' (83–4, 455). Along the way apple trees 'bow themselves to kiss the Pilgrims hands' (458); *Stillingfleet's replies*: '*Sibbs* Soliloquies' is presumably what Rochester wrote in 1674, and 'Stillingfleet's replies' is the emendation that he made after Stillingfleet's attack on the poem in the sermon preached at court on 24 February 1675. Stillingfleet had published three works with the word 'answer' or 'reply' in the title (Wing S5556, S5559, S5630), the most recent of which, *An Answer to Mr. Cressy's Epistle Apologetical*, was licensed for publication on 25 November 1674 (*T.C.* I 189) (Kristoffer F. Paulson, *PQ* 50 (1971), 657–63).

72–93 The attack on reason is punctuated by 'the repeated use of the contemptuous demonstrative', 'this' (Griffin 1973, 220).

75 *reason*: cf. 'the *Inward Light*, which is more properly called *Reason* . . . doth make us Capable of Converse with God' (Ingelo, *Bentivolio and Urania*, 2nd ed. (1669), ²177).

80–81 *doubt . . . finds them out*: cf. 'Is busy in finding *Scruples* out, / To languish in eternal *Doubt*' (Butler 1928, 38); *myst'ries*: the adversary uses 'mysteries' in the sense of 'religious truth known only from divine revelation' (*OED*); the speaker's 'mysteries' are verbal: paradoxes, Cretan Liars, non-referential abstractions ('a sense / Of something far more deeply interfused'), '*Accidents of Bread in Cheese*', oxymorons, quiddities, and the like.

86 *ointments*: cf. 'Witches . . . being carried through the Air, for which strange passage, they prepare their bodies with I know not what kind of oyntment; but I suppose it is made of the same ingredients, as that was, which turned *Lucian* into an Ass' (John Wagstaffe, *The Question of Witchcraft Debated* (1669), 31).

90 *philosopher*: Diogenes the Cynic (*c*. 412–323 B.C.) called Plato's lectures a waste of time. The tub story is in Diogenes Laertius, *Lives of Eminent Philosophers*, VI 23.

94–5 *action*: cf. 'il n'y a de réalité que dans l'action . . . il n'y a pas d'amour autre que celui qui se construit . . . un homme n'est rien d'autre qu'une série d'entreprises, qu'il est la somme' (there is no reality except in action . . . no love apart from acts of love . . . a man is no other than a series of undertakings of which he is the sum) (Jean-Paul Sartre, *L'Existentialisme est un humanisme* (1946), 55–8).

96 *happiness*: cf. 'Felicity is a continuall progresse of the desire, from one object to another; the attaining of the former, being still but the way to the later' (Hobbes 1935, 62; 'We hold these truths to be self-evident, that all men . . . are endowed by their Creator with certain unalienable rights, that among these are life, liberty and the pursuit of happiness' (*The Declaration of Independence*, 4 July 1776).

99 *right reason*: cf. 'right Reason constituted by Nature' (Hobbes 1935, 22); 'I alwaies love to keep a little *right reason* in the house' (Eachard 1672, 90–91).

100 *reason which distinguishes by sense*: nihil in intellectu quod non prius in sensu; cf. 'there is no conception in a mans mind, which hath not at first . . . been begotten upon the organs of Sense' (Hobbes 1935, 7).

102 *bounds desires with a reforming will*: in Hobbes's conception will is not the power of choice. Desires are bound by will only because will is 'the last Appetite, or Aversion' before action or avoidance (Hobbes 1935, 36). It is pointed out that 'This is behaviorism, and . . . that Rochester's . . . argument moves in another direction' (Reba Wilcoxon, *ECS* 8 (1974/5), 196).

109 *"What's o'clock?"*: cf. men 'that have no *Science*, are in better . . . condition with their naturall Prudence; than men, that by mis-reasoning, or by trusting them that reason wrong, fall upon false and absurd generall rules' (Hobbes 1935, 26). John Crowne may allude to these lines in *The Countrey Wit* (1675), 22: 'RAMBLE: The order of Nature . . . is to follow my appetite: am I to eat at Noon, because it is Noon, or because I am a hungry?' (Rochester 1984, 284).

115–16 *beasts . . . | As wise . . . and better*: elaboration of the familiar paradox that animals are intellectually and morally superior to man is the second major argument in Montaigne's 'Apology for Raimond de Sebond' (Montaigne 1700, II 182–250). One critic has observed that 'There is scarcely an idea . . . in [*A Satyr against Mankind*] that is not present in Montaigne' (Crocker 1937, 73).

120 *Meres*: 'man', the reading of the copy-text, may reflect a compositor's fear of *scandalum magnatum*, for Sir Thomas Meres was a prominent Whig politician.

122 *Jowler . . . wiser*: cf. 'Well might *an Antient Polish Bard* Decree, | *Jouler the Hound* a Wiser Beast than he [Sir Thomas Meres]' (Defoe, *The Dyet of Poland* (1705) (*POAS*, Yale, VII 114).

122–3 'the center [of the poem] is located physically in the blank space between lines 122 and 123' (David M. Vieth, *Language and Style* 5 (1972), 134).

125 *principles*: cf. 'The argument of orthodox morality is that man's principles restrain the excesses of his fallen nature. But in the *Satyr* those elements that would be identified as excesses of [fallen] nature (treachery, self-interest, and "wantonness" [l. 138]) are treated as principles' (Charles A. Knight, *MLR* 65 (1970), 258).

129–38 *beasts on each other prey, | . . . by necessity, they kill for food: | . . . they hunt | Nature's allowance . . . | But man . . . his fellow's life betrays, | . . . through . . . wantonness*: cf. 'L'Homme seul, l'Homme seul en sa fureur extrême | Met un brutal honneur à s'égorger soi-même' (Man alone in the extremity of his rage makes it a point of honour to cut throats) (Boileau, *Satire* VIII, 151–2); cf. 'When Beasts each other chase and then devour, / 'Tis Natures Law, necessity, / Which makes them hunt for food, & not for pow'r: / Men for Dominion, Art's chief vanity, / Contrive to make men die; / Whose blood through wantonness they spil' (Sir William Davenant, *The Cruelty of the Spaniards in Peru* (1658), 22) (Treglown 1976, 557); cf. Shadwell *The History of Timon of Athens, the Man-Hater* (*c.* January 1678; 1678) (Shadwell 1927, III 232) (K. E. Robinson, *N&Q* 218 (May 1973), 177); Defoe paraphrases these lines in *Serious Reflections during the Life and Surprising Adventures of Robinson Crusoe* (1720), 122–3, and William Empson writes his *Reflections from Rochester* around them (*Collected Poems* (1955), 54–5).

137–8 *With voluntary pains works his distress,* / *Not through necessity but wantonness*: Dryden turns these lines back on Rochester's *An Allusion to Horace*: 'what can be urg'd in their defence, who not having the Vocation of Poverty to scribble, out of mere wantonness take pains to make themselves ridiculous' (Dryden 1956– , XIII 14) (Paul Hammond, *N&Q* 233 (1988), 171).

140 *fear*: in Hobbes's state of nature there is 'no account of Time; no Arts; no Letters; no Society; and which is worst of all, continuall feare . . . therefore . . . [man] armes himselfe . . . [and] Force and Fraud, are . . . the two Cardinall vertues' (Hobbes 1935, 84, 85). The speaker has discovered that Hobbes's 'warre of every man against every man' persists into historic time (Griffin 1973, 237); in a brilliant society of arts and letters it has simply gone underground. Hobbes derives the *libido dominandi* from 'a generall inclination of all mankind, a perpetuall and restlesse desire of Power' (Hobbes 1935, 83, 63). Rochester derives it from fear. On the principle of Occam's Razor, Rochester's explanation is more elegant.

143 *fear . . . whence his best actions came*: cf. 'iura inventa metu iniusti' (justice was born of the fear of injustice) (Horace, *Satires*, I iii III).

155–8 quoted in John Dunton's *Athenian Sport* (1707), 265; Defoe rewrites l. 158, 'That all Men wou'd be Tyrants if they cou'd' (*The History of the Kentish Petition* (1701), 23) and then quotes it twice in the *Review* (6 September 1705, 9 April 1709) and thrice in *Jure Divino: A Satyr* (1706) (Introduction, p. 1, IV 4; V 18).

160 *knaves . . . in their own defence*: it has been said that the speaker urges men to be knaves (Griffin 1973, 244), but it seems that he only observes that knavery is necessary to survive in 'The rabble world' (l. 223) of seventeeth-century London.

162–3 *Amongst known cheats to play upon the square,* / *You'll be undone*: cf. 'gaming with a Sharper; if you cannot Cheat as well as he, you are certainly undone' (Swift 1939–68, III 37).

162–5 *Amongst known cheats . . .* / *The knaves will all agree to call you knave*: Defoe twice quotes these lines, apparently from memory, in the *Review* (17 March 1709, 23 October 1711). In addition he quotes l. 165 three times in the *Review* (13 March 1705, 7 April 1709 (Edinburgh), 13 May 1710). Lines 164–5 are quoted in Blount 1680, 81 (Manning 1986, 39).

173 *Who's a knave of the first rate*: quoted in Marvell's *Mr. Smirke or The Divine in Mode* (1676), 16, 'probably [published] in June [1676]' (Pierre Legouis, *Andrew Marvell: Poet, Puritan, Patriot*, 2nd ed. (1968), 202).

174 *All this with indignation*: cf. 'All this with indignation spoke' (Waller 1893, 88).

177 *False freedoms*: including the 'freedom' of the powerful to exploit the powerless (?).

179–219 These lines constitute one periodic sentence of the form 'If . . . if . . . then': If there is an honest courtier, if there is an honest churchman, then I'll recant my paradox. The structure of the sentence is obscured because the 'If there is an honest churchman' clause is cast in the form of a question, 'Is there an honest churchman?'

179–80 *if . . . there be | . . . yet unknown to me*: cf 'Faith in a woman (if at least there be / Faith in a woman unreveal'd to me)' (Giovanni Battista Guarini, *Il Pastor Fido*, trans. Sir Richard Fanshawe (1647), 27); *in* COURT *so* JUST *a* MAN . . . | *In* COURT *a* JUST *man* YET: the Ovidian 'turn', as Dryden called it, creates an effect like syncopation.

182 *ruin*: his most intimate advisers, beginning with Lady Castlemaine who told him he 'must rule by an Army' (Pepys, 29 July 1667), were urging ruinous policies upon the King.

188 *raise . . . his family*: as soon as Charles replaced the Cabal with Thomas Osborne, whom he appointed lord treasurer in June 1673 and created Earl of Danby in June 1674, Danby 'layes about him and provides for his family . . . It's wonderfull to see his good fortune in the marriage of his Children and settling his family in order; And many are of the opinion that when that is donne he will stop this Career' (*Essex Papers* 1890, 258, 260).

193 *blown up . . . prelatic pride*: cf. 'The aspirings that he [Rochester] had observed at Court, of some of the Clergy' (Burnet 1680, 120–21).

195–206 The prototypical churchman is guilty of all seven deadly sins: envy (l. 195), wrath (l. 197), avarice, pride, sloth, gluttony (l. 203), lechery (ll. 205–6).

210 *bishop*: 'possibly Thomas Barlow' (*Seventeenth Century English Poetry*, ed. John T. Shawcross *et al*. (1969), 608), consecrated Bishop of Lincoln in June 1675 at the age of sixty-nine. His skill in 'Casuistical Divinity' 'always leant to the side of his own self-interest' (*DNB*, I 1145). A better argument might be made for Gilbert Sheldon, Archbishop of Canterbury.

219 *Mysterious truths*: in the adversary's sense of the word 'mysteries' (80–81n. above), especially those in the Book of Revelation (?).

220–21 *If upon earth there dwell such God-like men, | I'll here recant my paradox*: cf. 'O, if the World had but a dozen Arbuthnots in it I would burn my Travells' (*The Correspondence of Swift*, ed. Harold Williams, 5 vols. (1963–5), III 104); *my paradox*: ll. 115–16).

223 *their laws*: as opposed to the 'rules' (l. 101) of right reason.

225 *Man differs more from man than man from beast*: cf. 'il y'a plus de distance de tel à tel homme qu'il n'y a de tel homme à tel beste' (there is more difference betwixt such and such a Man, than there is betwixt such a Man and such a Beast) (Montaigne 1700, I 439) (Crocker 1937, 71), i.e. average beast is superior to average man, maintaining the paradox (ll. 115-16); cf. 'a man hath no preeminence above a beast' (Ecclesiastes 3.19); 'when a Creature pretending to Reason, could be capable of such Enormities, he [the Master Houyhnhnm] dreaded lest the Corruption of that Faculty might be worse than Brutality itself' (Swift 1937–68, XI 232).

Plain Dealing's Downfall (Long time Plain Dealing in the haughty town)

It is tempting to connect these verses with Wycherley's last play, *The Plain Dealer* (December 1676; 1677), particularly since John Dennis records that Rochester and his friends 'by their loud approbation of it, gave it both a sudden and a lasting reputation' (Dennis 1939–43, II 277). But *The Plain Dealer* does *not* dramatize the proverb on which Rochester's poem is based. What is certain is that the proverb was current: 'Plain dealing is a jewel but they that use it die beggars' (Tilley P382) is quoted both in Shadwell's *Epsom Wells* (2 December 1672; 1673) and Wycherley's *The Country Wife* (January 1675; 1675) (Wycherley 1979, 319).

11 *trouble him no more*: cf. 'he from within shall answer and say, Trouble me not: the door is now shut' (Luke 11.7).

What vain, unnecessary things are men

This untitled fragment provides evidence of Rochester's compositorial practice. It was left unfinished in the midst of revision: the first draft is in ink, but ll. 8–10, 29–30, 33–4, and 53–4 are cancelled in pencil, and the three words of l. 55 are written in pencil (Rochester 1984, 195).

The fragment further breaks down into two pieces: in ll. 1–34 the speaker, a woman, complains that actresses have stolen the eligible men; in ll. 35–55 the same speaker petitions the actresses to make restitution. The paradox of the first line of the fragment is not sustained. Instead, the speaker explores one mishap of love from a woman's point of view: the introduction of actresses on the Restoration stage: 'To theatres . . . you are brought' (l. 47). The fragment is a sustained lucubration on the theme: a good man nowadays is hard to find.

5–7 *gave . . . crave . . . have*: the dissonant bump created by the imperfect rhyme emphasizes the sexual sense of 'have'. *OED* cites 'She's neither fish nor flesh; a man knowes not where to have her' (*1 Henry IV* (1598), III iii 133).

8–10 *the . . . playhouse . . . | To chaffer*: cf. 'The Playhouse is a kind of Market-place; / One chaffers for a Voice, another for a Face' (Dryden, Epilogue to John Bancroft's *Henry the Second, King of England* (8 November 1692; 1693); Dryden 1882–93, X 414); *women coursers*: cf. 'I am no Bawd, nor Cheater, nor a Courser / Of broken-winded women' (Beaumont and Fletcher 1905–10, V 303).

13 *Huff*: one of the vulgar guests in *Timon*.

14 *by*: the copy-text reading 'de' can be 'a dialectal (Kentish), foreign, or infantile representation of **The**' (*OED*), but 'the God' makes no sense in the context.

23–30 The lines constitute an elaborate metaphor: as my lady's frown drives away her Petrarchan lover and as 'th'insulting wife' (l. 27) drives her husband into the arms of his whore, so 'tyrannies to commonwealths convert' (l. 30). While it may be true that tyranny in marriage yields to the commonwealth of whoredom, in public affairs the opposite was held to be true: 'Tyrannies . . . spring naturally out of Popular Governments' (Sir William Temple, *Miscellanea: the First Part* (1680), 49).

24 *ends of plays*: in which boys get girls, and vice versa.

27–9 *th'insulting wife*: the domineering wife proverbially wears the breeches (Tilley B645), but in this case the hen-pecked husband gives the breeches to his whore, who wears them with 'gentler art' than the wife; *it*: probably 'mastery' (understood).

34 *please themselves*: cf. 'candle, carrot, or thumb'.

35 *kind ladies of the town*: in general, mock genteel for whores, but in the present context, actresses.

36–9 *men . . . | Poor broken properties that cannot serve*: cf. 'youth . . . / Too rotten to consummate the intrigue' (38.104–6); *properties*: 'any article (often an imitation) used as . . . a stage accessory' (*OED*).

46 *Rollo . . . Hart*: John Fletcher's *The Bloody Brother* (*c.* 1616; 1639) was one of the first Jacobean tragedies to be revived after the Restoration (14 August 1660) and was frequently played by the King's Company. The fratricidal brother, Rollo, Duke of Normandy, was played by Charles Hart. The fashionable women addressed in the poem could be assumed to know that Hart was an early lover of Nell Gwyn (whom he brought on the stage in 1665) and that Lady Castlemaine was 'mightily in love' with him (*BDAA*, VI 458; Pepys, 7 April 1668).

47 *you*: 'ladies of the town'/ actresses (l. 35).

49 *practise*: cf. 'Practis'd to Lisp, and hang the Head aside' (Pope 1939–67, II 183).

52 *idolators and atheists*: 'the beastly men' (l. 33) are idolators because they worship actresses, and atheists because they do *not* worship Love (l. 48).

54 *miracles*: cf. 'the pleasure he [Rochester] found in . . . calling the doing of Miracles, *the shewing of a trick*' (Burnet 1680, 87).

Consideratus, Considerandus (What pleasures can the gaudy world afford?)

Rochester presents a character that Samuel Butler did not write, the character of Il Considerato, the considerate man, in the original sense of the word 'considerate', 'thoughtful, deliberate, prudent' (*OED*). In Butler's practice the characters are described, whereas the character of Il Considerato, like that of his distant cousin Il Penseroso, is revealed by what he says. What he says makes him sound very much like a proto-Defoe:

> Thoughtfull without Anxiety,
>   And Griev'd without Despair,
> Chearfull, but without gayety,
>   And Cautious without fear.
>   (*RES*, n.s. 36 (1985), 351)

Title *Consideratus, Considerandus*: a thoughtful man who ought to be thought about.

28 [*Virtue*] . . . *Urged to be gone*: cf. 'Hence loathed Melancholy (Milton 1931–8, I i 34); 'Hence hated Vertue . . . Begone' (Oldham 1987, 58).

Scene i. Mr Dainty's Chamber (J'ai l'amour dans le cœur et la rage dans les os)

18 *posset*: Mistress Quickly makes a posset for Master Doctor Caius, hot milk laced with liquor and spices (*The Merry Wives of Windsor*, I iv 8).

The Maimed Debauchee (As some brave admiral, in former war)

Rochester wrote *The Maimed Debauchee*, Otway says, to give 'Bawdry' a bad name. And this may be the clue needed to identify the speaker. Like Falstaff he is the Vice of medieval drama. David M. Vieth's suggestion that *The Maimed Debauchee* might be entitled *In Praise of Debauchery* (Vieth and Griffin 1988, 20) comes into play here. The poem stands on its head the *Nichomachean Ethics*. What the Vice is saying and will continue to say is that excess is better than Aristotelian *mediocritas*. Blake says it 'leads to the palace of wisdom' (Blake 1957, 150). Rochester may not be so sure, for he does not conceal the price tag: 'pox . . . pains . . . scars . . . impotence'. For the thoughtful reader the poem may even stand as a cautionary tale: 'be wise' (l. 48), make love, not war.

Title *Maimed*: 'Mutilated, crippled, injured' (*OED* cites Bacon's *Essayes* (1625), 184: 'Hospitals for Maimed Soldiers').

1–24 The poem begins, like Donne's *A Valediction: forbidding Mourning* (1633) and Marvell's *An Horatian Ode upon Cromwell's Return from Ireland* (1681), with an extended epic simile.

1 *admiral*: Rochester served under two in the second Dutch War (1665–7), Sir Thomas Teddeman (?–1668) in the Bergen raid of August 1665 and Sir Edward Spragge (?–1673) in the Four Days' Battle of June 1666. Spragge, 'a merry man', sang catches with Pepys at Starkey's, admired Pepys's pretty neighbour, the widow Hollworthy, and left three illegitimate children upon his death in August 1673 (Pepys, 11 January 1666, 15 February 1666, 1 April 1667; Leneve 1873, 196).

1–12 cf. Lucretius, *De rerum natura*, II 1–6: 'Sweet it is, when on the great sea the winds are buffeting the waters, to gaze from land on another's great struggles . . . Sweet it is to behold great contests of war . . . when you have no part in the danger.'

9 *From his fierce eyes flashes of rage he throws*: cf. 'the anger came harder upon him [Achilles] / and his eyes glittered terribly under his lids,' (Homer, *The Iliad*, trans. Richmond Lattimore (1951), 392).

14 *wine's unlucky chance*: cirrhosis of the liver (?). The speaker is 'imagining future incapacities, not describing present ones' (Claude Rawson, *TLS*, 29 March 1985, 335). 18 *they*: 'new-listed soldiers' (l. 23).

27 *Vice*: 'Depravity . . . Personified' (*OED*); cf. 'that reverend Vice, that grey Iniquitie' (*1 Henry IV*, II iv 499).

28 *counsel*: cf. 'HARCOURT [to Horner] . . . . an old maim'd General, when unfit for action is fittest for Counsel' (Wycherley 1979, 288). *The Country Wife* opened at Drury Lane on or about 12 January 1675.

33–4 *tell of whores attacked (their lords at home), / Bawds' quarters beaten up and fortress won*: cf. 'Tell of towns stormed, and armies overrun, / And mighty kingdoms by your conduct won' (Waller 1893, 145) (Warren L. Chernaik, *The Poetry of Limitation: A Study of Edmund Waller* (1968), 198).

42 *incline*: 'some cold-complexioned sot' (l. 29) understood.

47 *Sheltered in impotence*: the paradox has been noted (Stuart Silverman, *Enlightenment Essays* 3 (1972), 210); *you*: 'hypocrite lecteur!' (T. S. Eliot, *Collected Poems* (1930), 72).

48 *good for nothing else*: Rochester may be mocking Edward Stillingfleet, who imagines the sinner's conscience telling him '*There is old Age coming, and when you will be good for nothing else, then will be time enough to grow wise and to repent*' (Stillingfleet 1675, 36; *be wise*: Pinto cites La Rochefoucauld, 'Les Vieillards aiment à donner de bons preceptes pour se consoler de n'estre plus en estat de donner de mauvais exemples' (No longer able to set bad examples, old men console themselves by professing good precepts) (*Reflexions ou sentences et maximes morales* (1665), 52) (Rochester 1953, 185), but the maimed debauchee professes bad precepts.

A Very Heroical Epistle from My Lord All-Pride to Doll-Common (Madam, If you're deceived, it is not by my cheat)

Title *Lord All-Pride*: Bajazet and Lord All-Pride seem to have been equally current as the nicknames of John Sheffield, Earl of Mulgrave. But since Marlowe's *Tamburlaine* (1590) was not revived during the Restoration, Etherege may have borrowed the name from Racine's *Bajazet* (1672) (Etherege 1963, 80–81); *Doll-Common*: the name of Cheater's whore in Ben Jonson's *The Alchemist* (1610). The historical Doll Common is Katherine Corey of the King's Company, who played the role in the revival of *The Alchemist* in December 1660 or December 1661 and regularly thereafter (*London Stage* I 44; Downes 1987, 15). She was arrested when she took off Lady Elizabeth Hervey in the character of Sempronia, an ageing courtesan (Pepys, 15 January 1669).

1 *Madam, If you're deceived, it is not by my cheat*: this line answers the rejected mistress's complaint: 'How far are they deceived who hope in vain / A lasting lease of joys from love t'obtain' (*Ephelia to Bajazet*, Etherege 1963, 9).

7 *In my dear self I centre everything*: cf. 'In him I centered all my hopes of bliss' (*Ephelia to Bajazet*, ibid.); cf. Dryden's dedication to Mulgrave of *Aureng-Zebe* (17 November 1673; 1676): 'True greatness, if it be anywhere on earth, is in private virtue; removed from the notion of pomp and vanity, confined to a contemplation of itself, and centring on itself' (Dryden 1882–93, V 194). George deF. Lord wonders where Dryden's tongue was when he wrote these lines (*POAS*, Yale, I 345).

17 *'tis as natural to change as love*: cf. 'Since 'tis nature's law to change, / Constancy alone is strange' (Griffin 1973, 60).

21 *blazing star*: cf. 'the Star by which I steered' (*Ephelia to Bajazet*, Etherege 1963, 10). In April 1674 Mulgrave was elected a Fellow of the Order of the Garter, the insignia of which includes a bejewelled star. But the primary reference is to Mulgrave's insistence that he is a 'blazing star' (comet) and the brilliant centre of admiration (*OED*), not the fixed star that the rejected mistress imagines.

22 *fatal*: comets appearing in December 1665 and March 1666 were followed by plague and fire in London.

23 *some great lady dies*: predictions that persons of great quality, 'especially Women', will die within the month are the stock-in-trade of astrology (Richard Saunders, *Apollo Anglicanus* (1676), sig. B2r; William Lilly, *Merlini Anglici Ephemeris: Or, Astrological Judgments for the Year 1677* (1677), sig. B3r). Adding 'great ladies' gives a further meaning to 'die'.

24 *The boasted favour*: cf. 'to you I brought / My virgin innocence' (*Ephelia to Bajazet*, Etherege 1963, 10).

25 *changing*: glossed 'making change', i.e. getting 'money of another kind (e.g. foreign or smaller coin) in exchange for money of some defined kind' (*OED*) (Rochester 1968, 114; Rochester 1984, 297), but Lord All-Pride may have in mind the proverb, Fair exchange is no robbery (Tilley C228).

37–8 *underneath the shade / Of golden canopies supinely laid*: cf. 'Underneath this Myrtle shade, / On flowry beds supinely laid' (Cowley 1905, 56).

45–6 *marks out the dame / Thou fanciest most to quench thy present flame*: cf. 'some brave Turk … beckons to the willing dame, / Preferred to quench his present flame' (Waller 1893, 87–8) (John Hayman, *N&Q* 213 (October 1968), 380–81).

53 *injured kinsman*: on 4 July 1675 Captain Percy Kirke challenged Mulgrave 'for haveing debauch'd & abus'd his sister', Mall Kirke, one of the maids of honour, even though 'shee herself does not accuse him … of getting the child … in which adventure the Earl of Moulgrave had the ill luck to receive a wound in his shoulder … this or something else has caus'd a 1000 storys to be rais'd about the father of the child' (Sir Richard Bulstrode, *The Bulstrode Papers* (1897), 304–5).

54 *midnight ambushes*: in September 1674 when Mulgrave won the favour of Mall Kirke, she was also mistress to the Duke of York and the Duke of Monmouth. As Captain of the Horse Guards, Monmouth, 'being jealous of Lord Moulgrave's courting his newest mistress', ordered Mall's lodgings in Whitehall to be watched. Mulgrave was arrested and confined to the guardhouse like a common trespasser (HMC *Rutland MSS.*, II 27).

56 *Damocles*: invited to occupy the seat of power of Dionysius, the tyrant of Syracuse (*c*. 432–367 B.C.), Damocles notices a sword hanging over his neck by a single horse hair (Cicero, *Tusculan Disputations*, V xxi 61–2).

To all Gentlemen, Ladies, and Others, whether of City, Town, or Country, Alexander Bendo wisheth all Health and Prosperity

'Being under an unlucky Accident, which obliged him to keep out of the way', Burnet says, '[Rochester] disguised himself, so that his nearest Friends could not have known him, and set up in *Tower-street* for an Italian *Mountebank*, where he had a Stage, and practised Physick for some Weeks' (Burnet 1680, 27). By impersonating Hans Buling, a Dutch mountebank practising in London, Rochester even found a role for his monkey. 'His first operations, which did not extend beyond the neighbourhood, were not particularly remarkable. But his reputation very soon spread to the other end of the town, and it was not long before the serving-maids at Court began visiting him, and the abigails of women of quality who, owing to the marvels which they reported of the German doctor, were presently followed by one or two of their mistresses' (Hamilton 1930, 258).

10 *Galenic*: Claudius Galenus (*c.* 130–200? A.D.) was the most celebrated medical writer of the classical era. His practice was based on physical rather than chemical medicine.

30–31 *I . . . have . . . courted these arts*: cf. 'I have beene at my book' (Jonson 1925–52, V 55).

42 *Qui alterum incusat probri, ipsum se intueri oportet*: Plautus, *Truculentus*, I ii 160. The text is corrupt but the meaning is clear: He who finds fault with others better be faultless himself.

50 *the counterfeit's . . . original*: Dr Alexander Bendo has two originals, Dr Alexander Fraser, one of 'the grand doctors of the court' (ll. 128–9), for his given name and medical specialties (urology and gynaecology), and Dr Hans Buling, one of 'the lesser quacks and mountebanks' (ll. 129–30), for his appearance.

112–15 *nay . . . humours . . . malignant*: cf. 'No, no . . . malignant humours' (Jonson 1925–52, V 52).

137 *Aretine's Dialogues*: the divine Aretino's *Dialogo* is the second part of *Cappricciosi e piacevoli Ragionamenti* (1534), partly translated into English as *The Crafty Whore: or, the Mistery and Iniquity of Bawdy Houses laid open* (1658).

139–40 *fits of the mother*: hysteria, cf. 'Oh how this Mother swels up toward my heart!' (*King Lear*, II iv 56).

185 *rare secrets*: cf. 'rare, and unknowne secrets' (Jonson 1925–52, V 54).

189–92 *when God . . . bestowed on man the power of strength and wisdom . . . it seemed but requisite that [woman] should be indued likewise . . . with some quality that might beget in him admiration of her*: cf. 'For contemplation hee and valour formd, / For softness she and sweet attractive Grace' (Milton 1931–8, II i 117).

197 *this my nine and twentieth year*: Rochester entered his twenty-ninth year on 10 April 1675.

210–11 *preserve your teeth white . . . as pearls . . . fastening them that are loose*: cf. 'seats your teeth . . . makes them white, as ivory' (Jonson 1925–52, V 57).

An Allusion to Horace. The 10th Satire of the 1st Book (Well sir, 'tis granted I said Dryden's rhymes)

In this poem Rochester invents the imitation as a new vehicle for satire. 'This mode of imitation', Johnson says, in which the ancients are familiarised, by adapting their sentiments to modern topicks, by making Horace say of Shakespeare what he originally said of Ennius, and accommodating his satires on Pantolabus and Nomentanus to the flatterers and prodigals of our own time, was first practised in the reign of Charles the Second by Oldham and Rochester.

(Johnson 1779–81, VII 184)

1 *rhymes*: by attacking Dryden's rhymed heroic drama, Rochester is also teasing Charles II, whose taste was partly formed by watching Corneille and Molière at the court of Louis XIV. 'The favour which heroic plays ... found upon our theatres', Dryden says, 'has been wholly derived to them from the countenance and approbation they have received at court' (Dryden 1882–93, II 285).

2 *stol'n*: 'for Comedy, he [Dryden] is for the most part beholding to French Romances and Plays, not only for his Plots, but even a great part of his Language; tho' at the same time, he has the confidence to prevaricate, if not flatly deny the Accusation, and equivocally to vindicate himself; as in the Preface to [*An Evening's Love; or,*] *the Mock Astrologer*: where he mentions Thomas Corneille's *le Feint Astrologue* because 'twas translated, and the Theft prov'd upon him; but never says One word of Molière's *Depit amoureux*, from whence the greatest part of *Wild-blood* and *Jacinta*, (which he owns are the chiefest parts of the Play) are stollen' (Langbaine 1691, 131).

3 *foolish patron*: the primary reference is to John Sheffield, Earl of Mulgrave, Rochester's *bête noir*, to whom Dryden dedicated *Aureng-Zebe* (17 November 1675; 1676), but Rochester includes himself in the satire for he had been Dryden's patron in 1671–3.

4 *blindly*: cf. 'Ben Jonson is to be admired for many excellencies ... but ... I do not admire him blindly' (Dryden 1882–93, III 243).

7 *paper*: i.e. paper of verses (Rochester 1982, 97). 'Horace is referring back to what he had written about Lucilius in *Satire* I iv' (Rochester 1984, 288).

9 *loose*: cf. 'I am sensible ... of the scandal I have given by my loose writings' (Dryden 1882–93, XI 231).

11 *Crowne's tedious scenes*: John Crowne's *The History of Charles the Eighth of France* (November 1671; 1672) is called 'a dull Rhiming Play' in the Epilogue (sig. L3v).

13 *false judgement*: cf. 'I ... am often vex'd to hear the people laugh, and clap ... where I intended them no jest; while they let pass the better things, without taking notice of them' (Dryden 1882–93, III 240).

13–14 *audience / Of clapping fools*: Dryden flatters his audience, attributing to 'the wit and conversation of the present age ... the advantage which we have above' Shakespeare, Jonson, and Fletcher (Dryden 1882–93, IV 242–3). Rochester does not flatter the Restoration theatre audience, calling them 'the rabble' (ll. 17, 120) and 'the vile rout' (l. 102) (Moskovit 1968, 453).

15 *thronged playhouse crack*: cf. 'Rochester ... was sensible, that [Dryden] deserv'd not that Applause for his Tragedies, which the mad unthinking Audience gave them' (Pseudo-St Evremond, Rochester 1707 (Bragge), sig. b7v).

17 *divert the rabble*: cf. 'he that debases himself to think of nothing but pleasing the Rabble, loses the dignity of a Poet, and becomes as little as a Jugler, or a Rope-Dancer' (Shadwell 1927, I 100).

18 *blundering*: cf. Settle's 'blundering hobling Verse' (*Notes and Observations on the Empress of Morocco* (1674), Dryden 1956– , XVII 89); 'a blund'ring kind of Melody' (ibid., II 74).

19 *puzzling Otway*: 'must refer to Otway's clumsy first play, *Alcibiades* (acted 22 September 1675), not to his highly successful second effort, *Don Carlos* (acted 8 June 1676)' (Vieth 1963, 158).

20 *due proportions*: cf. 'In all true Wit a due proportion's found, / To the just Rules of heighth and distance bound' (Shadwell 1927, II 291).

35–6 *Flatman ... rides a jaded muse*: whereas Cowley's '*Pindarique Pegasus*' is 'an unruly, and a *hard-Mouth'd Horse*, / Fierce, and unbroken yet' (Cowley 1905, 183); *whipped with*: at this uncertainty in the iambic cadence – is it 'WHIPPED with' or 'WHIPPED WITH'? – Flatman's Rosinante stumbles.

37–8 *Scipio fret and rave, / ... Hannibal ... whining*: P. Cornelius Scipio Africanus the Younger frets and raves very little in *Sophonisba. or Hannibal's Overthrow* (April 1675; 1676) (Lee 1954, I 103) and even for this Lee has a precedent in Livy XXVI xlix–l. But he had only poetic licence for a lovesick Hannibal (Lee 1954, I 87, 100, 106, etc.).

43 *hasty Shadwell*: Shadwell boasts that he wrote *The Miser* (January 1672?; 1672) in less than a month, *Psyche* (February 1675; 1675) in five weeks, and the last two acts of *The Libertine* (June 1675; 1676) in four days (Shadwell 1927, II 16, 279; III 21); *slow Wycherley*: Rochester's 'friends ... ought never to forgive him for commending them perpetually the wrong way, and sometimes by contraries' (Dryden 1882–93, V 337); 'Lord Rochester's character of Wycherley is quite wrong. He was far from being slow in general, and in particular, wrote the *Plain Dealer* in three weeks' (Spence 1966, I 37). 'The lyes in these Libels', Rochester tells Burnet, 'came often in as Ornaments that could not be spared without spoiling the Beauty of the *Poem*' (Burnet 1680, 26), or in this case the beauty of the contrast, 'hasty Shadwell and slow Wycherley'.

45 *force of nature*: cf. 'Trust Nature, do not labour to be dull' (Dryden 1956– , II 58).

54 *Waller ... for the bays designed*: John Dennis recalls Rochester's habit of 'repeating on every Occasion, the Verses of *Waller*, for whom that noble Lord had a very particular Esteem' (Dennis 1939–43, II 248) (Rochester 1984, 288).

58 *conquerors or ... kings*: Waller and Dryden both wrote panegyrics to Cromwell and to Charles II (Rochester 1984, 289).

59 *For ... satires ... Buckhurst*: Buckhurst's reputation for satire was based on *To Mr. Edward Howard on his Incomparable Incomprehensible Poem called The British Princes* (1669), one phrase of which, 'a strange alacrity in sinking' (Dorset 1979, 8), is the seed of luxuriant flowers in Pope.

60 *The best good man with the worst-natured muse*: cf. 'Never was so much ill nature in a pen as in his [Lord Dorset's], joined with so much good nature as was in himself' (Burnet 1724–34, I 264). Dryden, however, in his *Discourse concerning the Original and Progress of Satire* (1693), which he dedicated to Dorset, took 'strong exception' to this line, calling it 'an insolent, sparing, and invidious panegyric' (Dryden 1882–93, XIII 5; Farley-Hills, 1978, 221). It is doubtful that Dorset was pleased by this attack on his dead friend.

65–6 *impart / The loosest wishes*: Defoe, who wrote 'Some Account of the Life of Sir Charles Sedley' appended to Samuel Briscoe's edition of Sedley's works in 1722, found 'nothing indecent or obscene' in all that Sedley wrote (*The Works of the Honourable Sir Charles Sedley, Bart.*, 2 vols. (1722), I ⁸8).

71–3 *Dryden ... would be sharp*: cf. 'the snobbish delight with which Dryden reveals his social intimacy ... with the circle now known as the Court Wits' (William J. Cameron, in Love 1972, 282–3).

74 *he'd cry, 'Cunt'*: 'At *Windsor*, in the company of several persons of Quality, Sir

G[eorge] E[therege] being present ... When ask'd how they should spend the Afternoon ... *Let's Bugger one another now by G–d* ... was [Dryden's] smart reply' (Shadwell 1927, V 253).

75 *dry ... bob:* Drybob, a character in Shadwell's *The Humourists* (December 1670; 1671) who 'makes it his business to speak fine things', is a caricature of Dryden (Michael W. Alssid, *SEL* 7 (1967), 396–7; Winn 1987, 222–4).

76 *Poet Squab:* '*The Name given him* [Dryden] *by the Earl of Rochester*' (Shadwell 1927, V 254). 'Squab' refers primarily to Dryden's short, dumpy figure, like that of a fat pigeon, but in the context of dry bob (copulation without ejaculation) the term may imply sexual inexperience; a squab is also a newly-hatched chick.

77 *praise:* cf. Horace 'Praised *Lucilius* where he deserv'd it; *Pagina laudatur eâdem*' (Horace, *Satire* I x 4) (Dryden 1956– , XI 322, 527).

79–80 *Nor dare I ... tear | That laurel which he best deserves to wear:* the sincerity of Rochester's praise of Dryden seems guaranteed by the sincerity of Horace's praise of Lucilius (*Satire* I x 48–9) that these lines translate literally; *deserves:* because his 'talent ... can divert the rabble and the court' (ll. 16–17).

81–4 *Jonson dull; | Fletcher ... uncorrect ... Shakespeare ... | Stiff and affected:* cf. '*Jonson* did Mechanique humour show, | When men were dull ... *Fletcher* ... neither understood correct Plotting, nor that which they call *the Decorum of the Stage* ... *Shakespear* ... writes in many places, below the dullest Writer of ours, or of any precedent Age ... He is many times flat, insipid; his Comick wit degenerating into clenches, his serious swelling into Bombast' (Dryden 1956– , XI 201, 206, 212–13, XVII 55). Dryden did not, however, call Shakespeare 'Stiff and affected' (Winn 1987, 287).

84–6 *to his own ... | Allowing all the justness ... to these denied:* Rochester departs from his text here: Lucilius does not appropriate to himself the deficiencies he finds in Accius and Ennius: 'non ridet versus Enni gravitate minores, | cum de se loquitur non ut maiore reprensis?' (Does not Lucilius laugh at the verses of Ennius as lacking in dignity, though he speaks of himself as no greater than those he has blamed?) (Horace, *Satire* I x 54–5) (Moskovit 1968, 452).

85 *pride:* 'Rochester's ... emphasis on Dryden's pride, uses language taken from Dryden's recent criticism of himself' (Winn 1987, 287), e.g. 'Our author [Dryden] ... spite of all his pride' (Dryden 1882–93, V 201).

93 *Five hundred verses every morning:* cf. 'in hora saepe ducentos | ... versus dictabat' (Lucilius would often dictate two hundred verses in a morning) (Horace, *Satire* I iv 9–10).

96 *Mustapha:* cf. 351.114n.; *The English Princess:* presumably a slip of the pen for the failed epic of Dryden's brother-in-law, Edward Howard's *The British Princes: an Heroick Poem* (1668) (*DNB*, X 12; *Restoration Verse*, ed. Harold Love (1968), 299).

97 *composed in half an hour:* cf. 'This Poem [*Tyrannick Love, or The Royal Martyr* (1670)] ... was contrived and written in seven weeks', 'this play [*Amboyna, or The Cruelties of the Dutch to the English Merchants* (1673)] ... being contrived and written in a month' (Dryden 1956– , X 111; Dryden 1882–93, V 8). 130.43n.

102 *Scorn all applause the vile rout can bestow:* substitution of a spondee for an iamb in the fourth foot, 'Scorn ALL ap-PLAUSE the VILE ROUT CAN be-STOW', gives this line unusual emphasis, directing the reader to what may be the primary target of the satire, the Restoration theatre audience. The biographical fallacy (Ellis 1951, 1006–8) misleads readers into supposing that this line is 'the haughty snobbery of the Restoration aristocrat who despises *hoi poloi*' (Farley-Hills 1978, 203); it is in fact a critical commonplace (132.120).

111 *Betty Morris:* '*Buckhurst*'s whore' (*The Gentleman's Magazine*, May 1780, 218).

116 *squints*: cf. 'His [Scrope's] squinting looks' (Buckingham, *A Familiar Epistle to Mr. Julian, Secretary to the Muses* (1677, 57) (*POAS* Yale, I 398).

117 *censures*: none of Scrope's 'censures' of Rochester prior to 1676 are known.

120 *I loathe the rabble*: cf. 'Odi profanum vulgus et arceo' (I hate and shun the ungodly mob) (Horace, *Odes*, III i 1) (Rochester 1984, 290). What may be in the back of Rochester's mind is his belief (in Dryden's words) that 'The Court . . . is the best and surest judge of writing' (Dryden 1956– , XVII 4).

123-4 *And some few more . . . | Approve my sense*: the elitism is Horace's: 'paucorum hominum et mentis bene sanae' (a few friends and plain good sense) (*Satire* I ix 44). Defoe adapts these lines to his own purposes: 'Lord *Rochester* Answered a foolish Ignorant Censurer of his Works:

> If *Sackvill, Savil, Buckhurst, Wytcherly,*
> And some few more, whom I omit to Name,
> Approve my sense, I count your Censure FAME.'
> (*Mercator*, 28 November–1 December 1713)

Leave this gaudy, gilded stage

Ben Jonson's *Ode to Himself* (Come leave the lothed stage) addresses the 'vulgar censure' of his play *The New Inne* (1629; 1631) (Jonson 1925–52, VI 492–4). Rochester's poem addresses a third person, presumably an actress (Rochester 1968, 85). Besides the first line, Rochester borrows only the mock-Pindaric form of Jonson's poem.

Jonson's poem 'initiated a chain of responses by Randolph, Carew, "I.C.", and other poets, none of which approaches the independence of Rochester's proposal of a sexual alternative ("love's theatre, the bed") where Jonson resigned himself to the Alcaic lute' (Treglown 1973, 43).

Against Constancy (Tell me no more of constancy)

1 *Tell me no more*: six other seventeenth-century poems begin with this formula (Treglown 1973, 43).

7 *higher to advance*: see 97.16n.

20 *for worms*: 'to worms' is the reading of both the ms. copies, but J. L. Mackie argues for the more difficult reading of the copy-text: 'the poet is speaking of exchanging one mistress *for* another, and the appropriate antithesis to this is the notice of Fate exchanging [the poet] *for* worms, as if at some stage Fate should get tired of [the poet] and prefer worms instead. The notion of changing one thing *into* another is not strictly appropriate here' (*TLS*, 19 February 1954, 121).

To the Postboy (Son of a whore, God damn you, can you tell)

This is another report from the Maimed Debauchee (56), not in the person of the Vice, but in the person of the Ancient Mariner, compelled for penance to tell the tale of the 'hellish thing' that he had done. ' "To the Postboy" is a low-style equivalent of Horace's confessional satires, in which he honestly acknowledges his own moral shortcomings, thus enhancing the . . . authenticity of the satires' (Raman Selden, *English Verse Satire 1590–1765* (1978, 97).

1 *Son of a whore, God damn you*: cf. 'he [Rochester] could not speak with any warmth, without repeated Oaths, which, upon any sort of provocation, came almost naturally from him' (Burnet 1680, 152).

1–2 *can you tell / . . . the readiest way to Hell*: cf. 'can as eas'ly tell / How many yards and inches 'tis to hell' (Suckling 1971, I 68).

4 *Furies*: with whips of scorpions Tisiphone, Megara, and Alecto executed the vengeance of the classical gods.

5 *Sodom's walls*: defending a door against sexual aggressors, with the embattled constable of Epsom in the role of Lot, is common to the story of Sodom (Genesis 19) and the brawl at Epsom.

6–7 *or the college of Rome's cardinals. / Witness*: under the weight of the collective sexual expertise of the seventy-odd cardinals in the Sacred College, the iambic metre breaks down completely.

9 *fled*: it was said that in the Epsom brawl Rochester 'first ingaged & first fled and abjectly hid himselfe' (Marvell 1927, II 322).

10 *left my life's defender dead*: 'one of the strangest acts of contrition on record' (Vieth 1963, 201). 'Mr. Downs is dead. The Ld. Rochester doth abscond, and soe doth [George] Etheridge, and Capt. Bridges who ocasioned the riot Sunday sennight [18 June 1676]. They were tossing some fidlers in a blanket [cf. 'in *Epsom* Blankets tost' (Dryden 1956– , II 55) (Vieth 1963, 143n.)] for refusing to play, and a barber, upon the noise, going to see what the matter, they seized upon him, and, to free himself from them, he offered to carry them to the handsomest woman in Epsom, and directed them to the constables house, who demanding what they came for, they told him a whore, and, he refusing to let them in, they broke open his doores and broke his head, and beate him very severely. At last, he made his escape, called his watch, and Etheridge made a submissive oration to them and soe far appeased them that the constable dismissed his watch. But presently after, the Ld. Rochester drew upon the constable; Mr. Downs, to prevent his pass, seized on him, the constable cryed out murther, and, the watch returning, one came behind Mr. Downs and with a sprittle staff cleft his scull. The Ld. Rochester and the rest run away, and Downs, having noe sword, snatched up a sticke and striking at them, they run him into the side with a half pike, and so bruised his arme that he wase never able to stirr it after' (Hatton Correspondence, I 133–4). Downs died on 27 June 1676 (HMC *Seventh Report*, 467).

14 *blasphemed . . . God*: in Seneca's *Troas*, Act 2. Chorus (23) (?); *libelled kings*: in *On King Charles* (17) (?).

15 *ne'er stir*: the speaker's repetition of this injunction (l. 7) may indicate that the postboy is anxious to get away from this not-so-ancient mariner.

God bless our good and gracious King

'According to one source, these famous verses were "*Posted on* White-Hall-Gate". The antiquary Thomas Hearne describes them as "the lord Rochester's verses upon the king, on occasion of his majestie's saying, he would leave every one to his liberty in talking, when himself was in company, and would not take what was said at all amiss" [*Reliquiae Hearnianae*, I 119–20]. Still another account relates that "King Cha: praiseing the Translation of the Psalmes, Lord Rochester said Ile show you presently [i.e. right away] how they run"' [B.L. MS. Harl. 6914, f. 8v] (Rochester 1968, 134). Given Rochester's interest in '*the Sternholdian* Strain' (18, 110.176n.), the last account not only seems most likely but also recalls Johnson's parody of Thomas

Percy's ballad in similar circumstances (James Boswell, *The Life of Samuel Johnson, LL.D.*, ed. G. Birkbeck Hill and L. F. Powell, 6 vols. (1934-50), II 136n.). Rochester's epigram sounds like a parody of Sternhold and Hopkins's version of Psalm XIX:

> The fear of God is excellent
>   and doth endure forever:
> The judgments of the Lord are true,
>   and righteous altogether.
> (*The Whole Book of Psalms, Collected into English Metre* (1703), [sig. A5v])

2 *Whose promise none relies on*: cf. 'those princes have accomplished most who paid little heed to keeping their promises . . . Thus a prudent prince cannot and should not keep his word when to do so would go against his interest' (Machiavelli 1977, 49-50).

Love and Life (All my past life is mine no more)

These verses, like 'Fair Cloris in a pigsty lay' (10), versify the *Leviathan*:

> The *Present* onely has a being in Nature; things *Past* have a being in the Memory onely, but things *to come* have no being at all; the *Future* being but a fiction of the mind, applying the sequels of actions Past, to the actions that are Present.
> (Hobbes 1935, 11) (Treglown 1973, 44)

4-5 *images . . . kept in store | By memory*: cf. 'This *decaying sense* . . . wee call *Imagination* . . . But when we would express the *decay*, and signifie that the Sense is fading, old, and past, it is called *Memory*' (Hobbes 1935, 4); *alone*: the imperfect (fading) rhyme, 'are gone . . . alone', calls attention to fading memory.

14 *This livelong minute*: the phrase is much discussed. Tillotson glosses it 'the whole length of this minute', which seems clear and distinct (*Eighteenth-Century English Literature*, ed. Geoffrey Tillotson *et al.* (1969), 38). But Walker finds the phrase 'more paradoxical than this' (Rochester 1984, 251) and cites Treglown: '"This livelong minute" beguilingly echoes Christian descriptions of heaven, like Cowley's "Nothing is there *To Come*, and nothing *Past*, | But an *Eternal Now* does always last"' (Cowley 1905, 251) (Treglown 1973, 44). Perhaps the joke lies in applying 'livelong' ('An emotional intensive of *long*, used of periods of time. Chiefly in *the livelong day*, [*the livelong*] *night*' (*OED*)) to the short period of a minute, with a possible sidelong glance at 'the lucky minute' (9.^{1}23).

The Epilogue to Circe (Some few from wit have this true maxim got)

Sir William Davenant, who 'seemd contented enough to be thought [Shakespeare's] son' (Aubrey 1898, I 204), was poet laureate and first patentee of the Duke's Company. When he died in April 1668, his widow, Dame Mary Davenant, inherited the proprietorship of the company, which was then playing in the theatre at Lincoln's Inn Fields. Her eldest son, Charles Davenant (1656-1714), while still an undergraduate at Balliol College, Oxford, took advantage of the opportunity to write and produce an opera, *Circe*, for which John Banister wrote the music, Dryden the Prologue, and Rochester the Epilogue (Elizabeth Barry was in the cast).

4–5 *critics . . . agree | To loathe each play*: cf. 'All *Fools* have still an Itching to deride' (Pope 1939–67, I 243).

16 *And good for nothing would be wise at last*: cf. 'And being good for nothing else, be wise' (57.48). When a sound like 'laced' is expected, the imperfect rhyme 'last' heightens the scorn for dull critics who learn too late that ''tis . . . better to be pleased than not' (l. 2).

On Mistress Willis (Against the charms our ballocks have)

The news in June 1677 was that Thomas Colepeper, Baron Colepeper of Thoresby, had returned from Paris with his mistress. She was Sue Willis, 'whom he carry'd thither to buy whatsoever pleased her there and this nation could not afford' (*Savile Correspondence*, 62).

10–12 *beautiful, / . . . pert and dull*: the dissonance created by the imperfect rhyme calls attention to Willis's oxymoronic ugly beauty and dull mirth.

Song (By all love's soft yet mighty powers)

The Phillis in foul linen of this nasty song may have an historic counterpart: Rochester 'us'd the body of one Nell Browne of Woodstock, who, tho' she look'd pretty well when clean, yet she was a very nasty, ordinary, silly Creature' (Hearne 1884–1918, IX 79). The verses can be sung to the rollicking tune of 'Young Phaon', which John Banister Sr. wrote for a song in Charles Davenant's *Circe* (12 May 1677; 1677) (Simpson 1966, 811).

5 *be clean*: cf. 'Fair *Decency*, celestial Maid, / Descend from Heav'n to Beauty's Aid; / Though Beauty may beget Desire, / 'Tis thou must fan the Lover's Fire' (Swift 1937, 590).

14–16 *sinning; | . . . linen*: the imperfect rhyme provides an appropriately cacophonous close to the poem.

Upon Nothing (Nothing, thou elder brother even to Shade)

Rochester's '*Nothing* must be considered as having not only a negative but a kind of positive signification' (Johnson 1779–81, IV '11). The poem constructs a positive genealogy of Nothing:

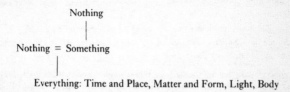

Nothing, of course, is androgynous. The Something that is 'Severed' from Nothing (l. 8) is female and their incestuous union produces Everything, an arrangement that exactly replicates the genealogy of Satan, Sin, and Death in *Paradise Lost* (Milton 1931–8, II i 61–9).

1 *Shade*: elemental darkness (Genesis 1.2); cf. '*Nothing* . . . is elder then darknesse' (Donne, *Essayes in Divinity* (1651), 35).

2 *the world was made*: cf. 'It pleased God . . . to . . . make of nothing, the World' (*The Humble Advice of the Assembly of Divines, Now by Authority of Parliament sitting at Westminster, concerning part of a Confession of Faith* (1646), 10).

6 *all proceeded*: cf. 'Here lies the inmost centre of creation, / From whence all inward forms and life proceed' (Henry More, *Psychozoia Platonica: or A Platonicall Song of the Soul* (1642),[1]17); *united what*: to make more obvious the pun on the pronominal use of 'what' and 'twat', the female pudendum (*OED*), Dunton prints 'the great united – *WHAT?*' (*Athenian Sport* (1707), 354); cf. 'In Prayse of a Twatt, By a faire Ladys Command' (Yale MS. Osborn f.b.66, f. 6).

7-9 *all*, / . . . *must* . . . *fall*: in Rochester's version of entropy, Nothing is 'fixed' (l. 3) but everything is in a state of flux tending toward dissolution into Nothing.

13-14 *Matter* . . . / *By Form assisted*: 'In Aristotelian and scholastic use: [matter is] That component of the essence of any thing . . . which has bare existence, but which requires the addition of a particular "form" to constitute the thing . . . as determinately existent' (*OED*, s.v. **Matter** *sb.*II, 6).

22 *mysteries*: cf. 47.67-9.

24 *truth*: one of Joseph Glanvill's 'Principles of Reason . . . that God hath implanted in our Souls . . . [is] *That nothing hath no attributes*' (*Logou Threskeia: Or, A Seasonable Recommendation, and Defence of Reason, in the Affair of Religion* (1670), 6-7).

27 *to be [nothing]*: cf. 'to be Nothing, is so deep a curse, and high degree of punishment, that Hell and the prisoners there, not only have it not, but cannot wish so great a loss to themselves, nor such a frustration of Gods purposes' (Donne, *Essayes in Divinity* (1651), 61).

33-6 *designs of state*, / . . . *least unsafe*: cf. *The Maimed Debauchee* headnote.

41 *princes' coffers*: Harold Love cites the stop on the Exchequer in January 1672 (Rochester 1984, 262), but the reference may be to later crises. In November 1677 when Louis XIV stopped the subsidies to Charles II for keeping England neutral in the wars on the Continent, Charles wept (Hutton 1989, 346).

45 *furs, and gowns*: worn by holders of civil, legal, parliamentary, or academic office (*OED*, s.v. **Gown**).

46 *French truth*: cf. 'Punic faith: . . . faithlessness' (*OED*, s.v. **Faith** 11b), treachery; *Dutch prowess*: cf. 'Dutch courage: bravery induced by drinking' (*OED* s.v. **Courage** *sb.* 4d).

50 *to thee they bend*: cf. 'Towards him [Satan] they bend' (Milton 1931-8, II i 55).

The Earl of Rochester's Answer to a Paper of Verses sent him by L[ady] B[etty] Felton and taken out of the Translation of Ovid's Epistles, *1680* (What strange surprise to meet such words as these)

1 *such words*: cf. 'Oft have I thirsted for a pois'nous draught, / As oft a death from some kind Ponyard sought; / Oft round that neck a silken Twine I cast, / Which once thy dear perfidious Arms embrac'd. / By death I'le heal my present Infamy, / But stay to choose the speediest way to dye' ('Phillis to Demophoon', *Ovid's Epistles, Translated by Several Hands* (1680), 96).

8 *sword and pen*: two of Ovid's heroines, Dido and Canace, write with sword in hand

(ibid., 8, 227); *pen . . . unfit* [for women]: cf. writing verse 'dangerous' [for women] (29.1–4).

12 *slain . . . revive*: cf. 'She smil'd to see the doughty Hero slain, / But at her Smile, the Beau reviv'd again' (Pope 1939–67, II 201).

Index of Titles and First Lines

CLICK ON A CLASSIC
www.penguinclassics.com
The world's greatest literature at your fingertips

Constantly updated information on over 1600 titles, from
Icelandic sagas to ancient Indian epics, Russian drama to
Italian romance, American greats to African masterpieces

•

The latest news on recent additions to the list, updated
editions and specially commissioned translations

•

Original scholarly essays by leading writers: Elaine Showalter
on Zola, Laurie R. King on Arthur Conan Doyle, Frank
Kermode on Shakespeare, Lisa Appignanesi on Tolstoy

•

A wealth of background material, including biographies
of every classic author from Aristotle to Zamyatin, plot
synopses, readers' and teachers' guides, useful web links

•

Online desk and examination copy assistance for academics

•

Trivia quizzes, competitions, giveaways, news on
forthcoming screen adaptations

•

eBooks available to download

READ MORE IN PENGUIN

In every corner of the world, on every subject under the sun, Penguin represents quality and variety – the very best in publishing today.

For complete information about books available from Penguin – including Puffins and Penguin Classics – and how to order them, write to us at the appropriate address below. Please note that for copyright reasons the selection of books varies from country to country.

In the United Kingdom: *Please write to* Dept EP, Penguin Books Ltd, Bath Road, Harmondsworth, West Drayton, Middlesex UB7 0DA

In the United States: *Please write to* Consumer Services, Penguin Putnam Inc., 405 Murray Hill Parkway, East Rutherford, New Jersey 07073-2136. *VISA and MasterCard holders call 1-800-631-8571 to order Penguin titles*

In Canada: *Please write to* Penguin Books Canada Ltd, 10 Alcorn Avenue, Suite 300, Toronto, Ontario M4V 3B2

In Australia: *Please write to* Penguin Books Australia Ltd, 487 Maroondah Highway, Ringwood, Victoria 3134

In New Zealand: *Please write to* Penguin Books (NZ) Ltd, Private Bag 102902, North Shore Mail Centre, Auckland 10

In India: *Please write to* Penguin Books India Pvt Ltd, 11, Community Centre, Panchsheel Park, New Delhi 110017

In the Netherlands: *Please write to* Penguin Books Netherlands bv, Postbus 3507, NL-1001 AH Amsterdam

In Germany: *Please write to* Penguin Books Deutschland GmbH, Metzlerstrasse 26, 60594 Frankfurt am Main

In Spain: *Please write to* Penguin Books S. A., Bravo Murillo 19, 1°B, 28015 Madrid

In Italy: *Please write to* Penguin Italia s.r.l., Via Vittoria Emanuele 45 1a, 20094 Corsico, Milano

In France: *Please write to* Penguin France, 12, Rue Prosper Ferradou, 31700 Blagnac

In Japan: *Please write to* Penguin Books Japan Ltd, Iidabashi KM-Bldg, 2-23-9 Koraku, Bunkyo-Ku, Tokyo 112-0004

In South Africa: *Please write to* Penguin Books South Africa (Pty) Ltd, P.O. Box 751093, Gardenview, 2047 Johannesburg